Male Sexuality

Male Sexuality

Why Women Don't
Understand It—
And Men Don't Either

Dr. Michael Bader

ROWMAN & LITTLEFIELD PUBLISHERS, INC.
Lanham • Boulder • New York • Toronto • Plymouth, UK

ROWMAN & LITTLEFIELD PUBLISHERS, INC.

Published in the United States of America
by Rowman & Littlefield Publishers, Inc.
A wholly owned subsidiary of The Rowman & Littlefield Publishing Group, Inc.
4501 Forbes Boulevard, Suite 200, Lanham, Maryland 20706
www.rowmanlittlefield.com

Estover Road
Plymouth PL6 7PY
United Kingdom

British Library Cataloguing in Publication Information Available

Library of Congress Cataloging-in-Publication Data:
Bader, Michael, 1952–
    Male sexuality : why women don't understand it—and men don't either /
Michael Bader.
        p. cm.
    Includes index.
    ISBN-13: 978-0-7425-6069-7 (cloth : alk. paper)
    ISBN-10: 0-7425-6069-4 (cloth : alk. paper)
    eISBN-13: 978-0-7425-6345-2
    eISBN-10: 0-7425-6345-6
    1. Men—Sexual behavior.
HQ28.B33 2009
306.7081—dc22   2008011335

Printed in the United States of America

♾™ The paper used in this publication meets the minimum requirements of
American National Standard for Information Sciences—Permanence of
Paper for Printed Library Materials, ANSI/NISO Z39.48-1992.

In loving memory of
Joseph Bader and Joseph Weiss

Contents

Acknowledgments

THIS BOOK EMERGED out of the conversations I had with dozens of male patients who consulted me after the publication of my first book, *Arousal*. I obviously can't mention them by name but want to thank them for their honesty and courage in addressing sexual matters that went to the core of who they were as human beings.

All the while I was writing this book, I was talking about the ideas in it with my teacher, therapist, and mentor, Joe Weiss. Joe was one of the most radical thinkers in the history of modern psychoanalysis, and his theories about personality and psychotherapy have changed the way that I and thousands of other therapists think about our patients. I owe him an enormous debt of gratitude for the ways he shaped my thinking and my life.

Lou Breger has not only been a tireless supporter of my work, but has demonstrated to me how to be mentored by a man in a way that makes one stronger.

Carl Sommers is not only a friend but the best editor I know. I want to thank him for the time he spent making this book more clear, readable, and persuasive. Deborah Kory reviewed this manuscript in detail and brought her extraordinary talent as an editor and intellectual to bear on making it better. And Rabbi Michael Lerner stood by this book during the many months it was seeking a home, helping me make contacts, reminding me of its value, and offering to excerpt it in his magazine, *Tikkun*.

This is the type of book that can fall through the publishing cracks, positioned as it is between trade and academic worlds. I want to thank Art Pomponio and his colleagues at Rowman & Littlefield for believing that a serious book about sexuality can not only be published in today's market but can and should be promoted to wider audiences.

Finally, I want to thank my wife, Margot. It is impossible for me to imagine producing anything of importance without her loving encouragement, sensitive and cogent feedback, and creative example. It is especially impossible for me to have written a book about male sexuality without other forms of her active participation.

Introduction

MALE SEXUALITY IS INCREASINGLY IN THE HEADLINES. Not only are we privy to the infidelities of male politicians and entertainers, but now the details of their sexual practices are also in the public domain. Elliot Spitzer likes to play with high-class hookers, Bill Clinton with cigars, Dick Morris with feet, Bill O'Reilly with phones, James McGreevy with men, Hugh Grant with transvestites, and Larry Craig likes playing footsie in bathroom stalls. Further, with the rise of the Internet, the debates of the 1980s about pornography have resurfaced. Since sexual stimulation is now only the click of a mouse away, alarms are being sounded about the dangers lurking in cyberspace. Children are allegedly getting exposed to extreme forms of adult sexuality and losing their innocence. Pedophiles are trolling chat rooms for potential victims. Cybersex addiction among men is a growing problem, imperiling their marriages and mental health. And since the overwhelming majority of consumers of Internet pornography are men, the easy availability of images that objectify and devalue women allegedly reinforces the most misogynist tendencies in men and makes them even less available for real intimacy.

If we understood the real dynamics of male sexuality, these controversies would suddenly appear in a different light. Fetishes are not some bizarre sexual interest but are common and easily understandable. Most men will never get addicted to cybersex, and their enjoyment of it does not necessarily threaten their relationships or reinforce negative attitudes toward women. The outcry about the dangers of the Internet is exaggerated and being used as a Trojan horse to promote censorship and more strictly regulate normal sexuality. Based on thirty years of clinical experience, my aim in this book is to present a new theory of male sexuality that will call

1

into question all of the stereotypes, caricatures, and "common-sense" assumptions that we all hold about the erotic lives of men today.

Our ability to understand the differences between sexual fantasy and reality is crucial but increasingly under attack. The unconscious mind was one of Freud's great discoveries, and its central tenet was that manifest behavior and conscious aims are often merely the tip of the iceberg of meaning, obscuring a deeper and more authentic truth. We are in danger of turning back the clock to pre-Freudian days, flattening and cynically dismissing the deeper motivations that really make people tick.

This book is an attempt to return some sense and meaning to our understanding of sexuality and, in particular, of male sexuality. At the same time that we resuscitate the importance of the unconscious mind, however, we have to keep our eye on the fact that the underlying feelings that animate much of male sexuality are, in fact, cultural problems with complicated historical roots. Understanding the social context in which male sexuality is formed will deepen our compassion for men and underscore the ways that our culture isolates them and burdens them with too much responsibility. There is a vital need for a model of sexuality that explains the intimate connections between the personal and unconscious lives of individuals and the broader backdrop of changes in family life, gender roles, and cultural norms.

This is a book about the value of understanding. It assumes that when we oversimplify male sexuality or demonize any form of it, everyone suffers. It assumes that when men understand themselves, they feel less shame, and that when women understand men, they feel more connected to men and more compassionate. And it assumes that when both men and women understand how the world shapes and hurts their sexuality, they are more equipped to change it.

The Secret Logic of
Male Sexuality

THERE IS AN ADAGE THAT SAYS, "Men use love to get sex, while women use sex to get love." Women's sexual needs are thought to involve meaning, while men are apparently obsessed with sex for its own sake. A woman patient of mine put it more graphically when, while complaining about her husband, she quipped, "All you have to do to make a man happy is to feed him and fuck him. They just have different needs than women." When I repeat this to public audiences, both women and men generally laugh. As Billy Crystal once joked, "Women need a reason to have sex. Men just need a place."

But do men only want one thing? Is male sexual desire so simple and straightforward that it can be reduced to a joke? Perhaps—but only if you take what men say and do at face value. If you look beneath the surface, read between the lines, a completely different reality emerges. The stereotype of men "thinking with their little heads rather than their big heads" is not only wrong but also harmful. It leaves women bewildered and frustrated about what men really want (or don't), leads men to feel privately ashamed or guilty about their sexual fantasies and urges, and stifles communication between the sexes.

Drawing on over thirty years of clinical experience working with men around sexual issues, my aim is to debunk myths and unmask truths about male sexuality. At their deepest level, most men don't see women as things or conquests; they actually worry about them—worry too much, in fact. They aren't too selfish but too guilty. They aren't predatory but lonely. They may seem to have more power than women but usually feel as if they have less. And the real reason that men sometimes put women down is to not feel put down themselves.

Armed with an accurate picture of what really motivates men in the bedroom, women will feel less provoked and bewildered by their partners and, therefore, will more comfortably feel compassion. Men will develop a more genuine sympathy for the issues with which they struggle and be able to talk about them more freely. When stereotypes about male sexuality are replaced with true understanding, both genders benefit.

The Hidden Dynamics behind Human Sexuality

Before we identify what is special about male sexuality, we need to first consider what is universal. Most important is that sex begins in the mind and travels down, not vice versa. Consider for a moment why the slightest brush of an earlobe by a lover's lips can be tremendously exciting while direct genital contact during a medical exam leaves us cold. The difference lies in the meaning of the events, and meaning is constructed by our minds, not our erogenous zones.

For both sexes, then, the journey of sexual desire is not that of a simple reflex. Between our innate desire and biological capacity for pleasure and connectedness and the particular forms that it takes in the lives of individual men and women lies a psychic system that either allows sexual excitement to flourish or shuts it down completely. This "system" is unconscious and can be a minefield for sexual desire.

At the deepest level of our minds, we all have feelings and beliefs that complicate sexual excitement. For example, many of us tend to feel especially guilty and worried about others. As we will see, such feelings are incompatible with the sense of selfish abandon necessary for the human mind to become sexually excited. Others feel vulnerable to feelings of shame and rejection or are prone to feelings of inadequacy, and such negative states invariably have a chilling effect on desire. Suffice it to say that human beings are wired such that we cannot get maximally aroused while we're feeling overly responsible for others, worried about their welfare, sensitive to shame and rejection, or depressed about ourselves.

And yet who among us never felt guilt or rejection? While the desire for pleasure is universal and the capacity to feel it may be hard-wired, everyone has some mixture of the very feelings and beliefs that make sexual excitement potentially problematic.

Notice that I said *potentially* problematic. The same mind that creates a problem for sexual excitement also provides—courtesy of the imagination—a potential solution. We see such solutions all around us: they are called sexual fantasies and sexual preferences. Sexual fantasies and preferences are the vehicles by which our minds counteract the chilling effect of feelings of guilt, worry, shame, rejection, and helplessness and make it safe enough to experience pleasure. For example, one patient of mine liked to have the lights out during sex to reduce feelings of shame about his body. A dark bedroom was the condition in which he could feel safe enough from feelings of shame to become aroused. Another preferred sex from the rear to eliminate eye contact and, therefore, reduce the danger of having to worry about whether his sexual partner was satisfied. A third person preferred the opposite—continual eye contact—in order to get a certain type of reassurance against a perceived danger of rejection or abandonment. A fourth was especially drawn to younger women because he imagined that their youth represented happiness and optimistic energy and, therefore, would counteract his own chronic and exaggerated sense of obligation to make women happy. A fifth had to imagine being sexually dominated to surrender the psychic burden of feeling too responsible, too "in charge." And still another fantasized about a sexual liaison with a popular media personality whose effervescent personality somehow lifted the lid that had been holding back that patient's sexual excitement.

These sexual scenarios were solutions to problems. We all have some version of these problems, and we all develop just the right solutions in our quest for sexual pleasure. An example from my own adolescence further illustrates this point. When I was fifteen years old I had a crush on a girl who, in retrospect, probably felt the same way. However, she was shy and I was nervous and guilty about being sexually assertive. I remember walking her home one night thinking desperately to myself that I should just take her hand or put my arm around her and yet felt paralyzed and couldn't do it. What was I afraid of? Well, rejection, of course. But when I think back on that situation, I realize that my fear of rejection rested on two irrational and entirely unconscious assumptions: first, that girls would naturally tend to feel intruded on and burdened by my sexual interest. And second, that for some reason of which I was not aware, I somehow wasn't supposed to be romantically assertive. Both beliefs had a rather chilling effect on my libido.

In the context of my family of origin, however, such beliefs made perfect sense. My mother was frequently irritable and unhappy and clearly resented my father (often with good reason). Like most children, I grew up with the unwitting assumption that the sensibilities I saw in my mother were lying just beneath the surface in all women. In this case, I generalized from my mother and developed the secret belief that women were prone to disappointment in men and in life, a sensibility that I inferred would hardly be welcoming to male sexual overtures. My sexual confidence suffered as a result.

At this time in my life my favorite television show was *I Dream of Jeannie*. The story line was simple: astronaut Tony Nelson's rocket veers off course and lands on a deserted island where he finds a bottle, which, when rubbed, calls forth a genie. Only this genie—named Jeannie—is a cute bubbly blond woman wearing a harem outfit. Jeannie's job is to make her master happy, and though Tony frequently becomes cranky and embarrassed by Jeannie's antics, she always remains cheerful, confident, and loyal. I had a passionate crush on Jeannie and, in my fantasy life, suffered none of the inhibitions that I evidenced in reality.

In this simple vignette lay not only a window into my own psychology but all the makings of a new theory of sexuality. In fantasy, Jeannie counteracted my fears and irrational beliefs about women. She was sexy and wanted nothing more than to please her man. There was no risk of offending her or being rejected. My fantasy girlfriend positively wanted me to be strong. I was drawn to the exact fantasy scenario that temporarily negated my guilt about being sexually assertive with women.

If we look beneath the simple surface of sexual arousal, we find a complicated psychological process of which most of us are completely unaware. People get sexually aroused only if their imaginations find a way to temporarily negate or overcome their psychological roadblocks to pleasure. The value of this approach to sex lies not only in its ability to explain the meaning of someone's particular fantasies and behavior but also to reveal his or her most important emotional conflicts. If sexual fantasies and desires emerge as solutions to psychological problems, and if those problems involve core fears and conflicts, then sexuality becomes a powerful window through which we can view the workings of the mind. Freud said that dreams were the "royal road to the unconscious." I would argue that we get there faster by studying sexual fantasies.

By decoding our sexual fantasies and preferences, we can uncover what makes us tick as human beings. Sexuality and psychology, then, are like a key and a lock—by understanding the shape of the key, we can infer a lot about the contours of the lock it opens. Since sexual arousal can arise only when a psychic problem has been temporarily "solved" by a fantasy, the study of fantasies is really a study of the twists and turns of the deepest levels of the psyche.

By fantasies I am not only referring to the private daydreams and preferred narratives that we use to arouse ourselves. I am using the concept of fantasy to include all of our sexual preferences, all of the erotic conditions to which we seem to gravitate. Thus, while an individual's sexuality takes many forms, the underlying meaning is always the same. Whether the person's sexual arousal is a response to a picture, person, sexual position, or elaborate daydream, it derives from the same set of psychological dynamics.

For example, when my patient Donald masturbated, he often thought of having sex with the singer, Madonna. He was drawn to images of her wearing boots with stiletto heels and a brassiere creating sharp conical breasts. We came to understand that such a representation was arousing to Donald because it symbolized a type of hard strength in relation to which he could "let go" of the customary feelings of responsibility, vigilance, and worry with which he usually approached women. Donald's masturbation daydream certainly fit the conventional definition of sexual fantasy. However, Donald was also attracted to any depiction of strong or sexually confident women. He expressed such a preference in the pornography he enjoyed. He liked women who appeared physically strong and sturdy. He preferred women to take charge in the bedroom. Each of these situations might have felt subjectively different to Donald, but the excitement connected to each came from the same psychological sources. *Sexual preferences are merely sexual fantasies that are enacted in the external world.*

If both men and women get aroused by finding creative ways of counteracting their inhibitions and fears, what accounts for the obvious differences between the genders? The answer is that men face special inhibitions around their sexual desires and use special psychological techniques to overcome these inhibitions. For example, we will see that in the course of growing up, men develop a particular form of guilt toward women that interferes with their ability to "let go" sexually, and that they "solve" this problem through objectifying women and by splitting sex from intimacy. In addition, we will learn that men often suffer from a special type of loneliness in our culture and that such feelings interfere with their sexual desire. Certain types of pornography and cybersex offer men a highly specific antidote to such feelings. We will examine every common manifestation of male sexual behavior through this same lens.

Clinical Examples

My patient Joe loved pornography. Joe had a large collection of adult magazines; he once told me with pride that his collection of *Penthouse* magazines was complete. He called phone-sex lines and frequently surfed the Internet for porn that not only included still photos and videos, but interactive sex as well. He paid for one-on-one live sessions with porn stars and joined bulletin boards and chat rooms that specialized in sexual conversation. Additionally, Joe regularly visited massage parlors and escort services to have sex with prostitutes.

It might seem that Joe spent all of his time thinking about or having sex, but this was not the case. Joe was an attorney, married to a woman whom he loved but toward whom his sexual ardor had diminished over the years. His wife was aware of some parts of his sexual "hobby"—she tolerated his magazine collection—but was unaware of the rest. Joe had friends, was active politically, and was widely respected in his community. However, he had always had a special need for, and an appreciation of, underground sexual practices.

Joe was both a typical and atypical American male. He was typical in the sense that men are the overwhelming consumers of pornography, cybersex, and sex-for-hire. Joe's involvement in pornography and Internet sex was excessive, but hardly outside the mainstream of male sexual behavior in the United States. Given a sex industry with yearly revenues of $12 billion and a society in which 30 million men log on to pornography websites regularly, Joe's obsession with porn and prostitutes was simply an extreme version of common male interests. What was atypical about Joe was both the intensity of his extramarital sexual activity and the fact that he was highly insightful about his motivations.

Joe experienced his life as fairly grim. "I do well at life," he once told me in a forlorn voice, "but I don't enjoy it very much." He was successful in his job, marriage, and friendships, but deep down his life was an unending strain. Joe felt responsible for all his social interactions, down to the briefest interaction at a cocktail party. He once told me that he had the fantasy that if he was in the middle of a conversation with a group of people and had to leave for a minute, everyone would have left when he returned. In other words, Joe said, he felt he was the glue that held everything together, that he was responsible for everyone and everything. In his mind, he was supposed to make his wife happy, as well as his clients at work. And it wasn't easy to please other people—it took work. He would come home from cocktail parties drained and depleted because he had put so much effort into being "interesting."

His sexual journeys, however, were a vacation from this life of toil. He explained what it was like when he hired a prostitute:

> It's like I'm the center of her attention. I don't have to do anything in particular, but I can do anything I want and it's just fine with her. You can't believe what it's like to be with someone and to have your satisfaction the only focus for both of you. I can totally surrender to my feelings and totally get into my pleasure without thinking for even a moment about her feelings and needs.

That Joe got to act out his innermost fantasies with a prostitute isn't very noteworthy. After all, that's the point of going to a prostitute. What is worth noting, however, is the centrality of responsibility—or in this case, its absence. With a woman he hired, Joe did not have to worry about his partner at all, and instead could be utterly selfish. These women offered Joe the opportunity to be the center of attention, to feel entitled to pleasure on his terms alone, and to not have to pay for it in any way other than with money. Paying for sex enthralled him because it solved a problem, counteracting his irrational feelings of guilt and worry about others.

The experience of being selfishly indulged without any expectation of reciprocity had been almost nonexistent in Joe's earlier life. To everyone but Joe, his mother was the life of the party. Sociable, generous, and brilliant, she seemed to his friends like an ideal mother. But when outsiders weren't around, she was often depressed. Today, she probably would have been diagnosed as bipolar, rapidly cycling between emotional highs and lows. She had given up a promising career as an actress to marry Joe's father, and she brought her theatricality to the family drama. But like an actress who comes alive only when on stage, Joe's mother went into an emotional slump when she wasn't performing. She mechanically performed the tasks of mothering, but Joe always sensed that it was a role she didn't enjoy. In fact, he felt that she was burdened by it.

Of course as a child Joe couldn't really know all of this consciously. He worried about his mother and tried either to comfort her or stay out of her way. But inevitably he would retreat to his room, feeling quite sad. Based on these experiences with his mother, Joe developed a deep—albeit unspoken—belief that he wasn't easy to love or care for, that his needs for such love and care burdened other people. He grew up with the sense that women in particular would always take more than they gave. Joe's father, on the other hand, was an alcoholic who became surly and mean when he drank. Joe and his mother would bear the brunt of his drunkenness in the evenings. This only led Joe to feel even sorrier for his mother and more unprotected and rejected.

Because both parents put a lot of stock in appearances, Joe, like his parents, developed a successful career and public personality that completely concealed the emotional desolation he privately felt. At the deepest level, Joe was, in fact, desperate to be loved, but unconsciously believed that this could occur only if he sacrificed himself, not if he expressed his own needs and desires.

Before his marriage, Joe flirted with women, but when it came to initiating sex with them, he often ran away. Casual sexual encounters in which the only expectation was that both parties have fun made him intensely uncomfortable because he couldn't let himself imagine that women could enjoy such superficial mutuality. He allowed himself to enjoy the fantasy that he was making a woman feel good by being charming and attentive, but when it came down to having his own needs met via actual sex, he would feel guilty and anxious. When he eventually married, Joe felt less guilty about satisfying himself in bed because he imagined that the security of the relationship was reassuring to his partner.

Joe liked and needed the stability and security of an intimate relationship, but his overwhelming feelings of responsibility had a chilling effect on his libido. In long-term relationships, Joe in effect re-created his relationship with his mother and began to feel more like a caretaker than a lover—a caretaker who at bottom was lonely and unloved. Eventually, he found a solution—albeit a transient one—to this problem, namely, pornography and prostitution.

When Joe told me about his encounters with prostitutes or his interactions with lap dancers or his Instant Messenger cybersex, there was a poignancy about his descriptions. In speaking of a sexual massage he had recently received, he made comments like "It was all for me" or "I could just lie back and enjoy myself" or "She enjoyed everything and anything that I wanted to do with her body." It became evident that Joe believed a "normal" woman could never make his needs the center of her attention, but instead would invariably require that he sacrifice his own interests to please her. No wonder he preferred women who were paid to please him or cyberpartners who fit exactly into his preferred sexual fantasies. Only in these settings could Joe be himself.

If Joe's wife were to find out about his sexual infidelities, she would of course feel rejected and devalued and wouldn't be wrong to feel this way. She would likely experience Joe as selfish and irresponsible. And while her judgments about Joe's character would be understandable, they would also be, at best, incomplete and, at worst, incorrect. Joe suffered from an inordinate amount of responsibility, not a lack of it. He was not too selfish but too inhibited about feeling selfish. He was not fundamentally insensitive to the feelings of women but overly worried about them. Joe's problem was that his capacity to feel passionately joyful with a woman he loved was so inhibited by irrational feelings of guilt and responsibility that he sacrificed his own needs on the altar of others'. The sexual solutions he sought reflected his desperate loneliness and resignation that things could ever be different.

Pathogenic Beliefs

Joe's wife would have every right to feel hurt and furious as a result of Joe's sexual behavior. No one is obliged to be "understanding" when he or she is hurt, and yet for those who want to understand the sexual behavior of a partner, it is crucial to look at such behavior as the tip of an iceberg, as a sexual solution to problems that are not primarily sexual. The logic is simple: since sexual arousal can occur only if internal blocks are overcome, then it is these blocks that hold the key to understanding sexual desire. Sexual behavior is like a road. While its planners have a destination in mind, by and large the shape of the road is determined by the terrain on which it is built. Steep hills call for the road to wind, rivers for the construction of a bridge or tunnel. The forms that sexuality takes, the ways it is consciously experienced and perceived, are the result of a similar adaptation, in this case to an underlying psychic terrain.

Joe, like all of us—all the time—was unconsciously working to overcome internal obstacles to pleasure and fulfillment. Like most men, he felt hyper-responsible for women and was prone to guilty worries about hurting them, a set of emotion-laden assumptions that interfered with his ability to "let go" and surrender to the full force of his passion. However, he was consciously aware only of his attraction to pornography and prostitutes, not the underlying emotional blocks to which his sexual preferences were a response. The real meaning of Joe's behavior can be plumbed only by examining his worries about women and his belief that he was responsible for them.

In the 1980s the psychoanalyst Joe Weiss coined the term *pathogenic beliefs* to describe the feeling and attitudes that interfere not only with sexual pleasure but with happiness in general. When physicians call something a pathogen, they mean that it causes a disease or disease process. Similarly, a belief is pathogenic if it causes something psychologically unhealthy—in this case, the inhibition of a normal and healthy desire and goal. Weiss argued that all children normally develop pathogenic beliefs that often last a lifetime in response to their family environments.

Usually formed in childhood, a pathogenic belief is based on the assumption that if people pursue a normal aim or pleasure—for example, sexual passion, emotional independence, or the pride of being the center of attention—the relationship with their parents will somehow be threatened. Since the tie to caretakers is of life-and-death importance to a child, the troublesome aim or pleasure is relinquished. Weiss insisted that such inhibitions be called beliefs and not simply feelings because, he argued, our feelings never stand alone but are always embedded in a certain conception of the world. Pathogenic beliefs are deeply felt elemental conceptions about the nature of reality and our relationship to that reality.

For both men and women, pathogenic beliefs are the primary impediment not only to sexual pleasure but to satisfaction in every area of life. For example, a patient of mine felt so guilty about hurting his mother with his assertiveness that he became meek and deferential. The guilt was unconscious—the only feeling he was aware of was insecurity. His guilt, though, was based on a general view of his mother as weak and especially threatened by male assertiveness, as well as an exaggerated sense of his own power to harm her. When he eventually became aware of his feelings, it was in the context of becoming aware of his broader assumptions—his pathogenic beliefs—about his mother and himself.

Another patient grew up in a family in which she sensed that her parents were weak and lacked confidence in their own authority. Such a perception is disturbing to children who long for parents firm enough to provide an emotionally safe environment with good boundaries. My patient developed the pathogenic belief that she could overwhelm her parents with her needs and responded by frequently getting into trouble in ways that invited her parents to act strong and discipline her. Acting out didn't reflect a true loss of control but, instead, an implicit invitation to her parents to step up to their responsibilities. As a result of her experience in her family and the pathogenic beliefs to which it gave birth, she sabotaged herself to restore at least the illusion of secure parents and parenting.

Pathogenic beliefs are not conscious abstract theories about the world, but emotionally charged and usually unconscious frameworks that children naturally form to make sense of the world around them. We all have them. They cause us trouble but don't necessarily mean we are mentally ill. All children are highly motivated to adapt to reality, especially their familial reality as they see it, and no family is perfect. Thus, if their mother appears unhappy, children automatically take responsibility and do whatever they can to help her, even if that involves hurting themselves. Unfortunately, such beliefs don't disappear when we grow up, but remain buried.

By buried, I mean unconscious. Pathogenic beliefs are not consciously held opinions. Such beliefs don't ever feel as if they're "learned" in the same sense that a child learns not to touch a hot skillet. Pathogenic beliefs don't feel so much chosen as woven into the fabric of the world. We don't learn about gravity; it just is. Similarly, we don't learn that we're unlovable or that we're responsible for taking care of a parent; such beliefs, like breathing, are simply facts of life.

Pathogenic beliefs are often made unconscious because they are too painful or frightening to contemplate consciously. If a child is neglected and responds by feeling that it's his fault because of something toxic in him, then both this problem and solution have to be made unconscious. If it were not, the child might have to become more explicitly aware of the pain of being ignored, as well as the intolerable knowledge that people who are supposed to love him do not. As long as the child takes responsibility for the trauma, and keeps both the real trauma and his or her reaction to it unconscious, that child doesn't have to face reality.

In the course of development, all of us form pathogenic beliefs. For example, my patient Sheila was abandoned by her mother when she was three years old and left in the care of a distant father and a stepmother who resented her. Sheila acquired the pathogenic belief that all people were like her mother and would invariably feel burdened by any display of dependency and reject her for it, just as she had imagined her mother had done when she abandoned her. Sheila had developed the pathogenic belief that if she had been an "easier" child, her mother would not have left. As Sheila grew up, she was reluctant to depend on anyone and was extremely sensitive to rejection, but she felt entirely justified in her guardedness, blaming other people who regularly disappointed her. Her pathogenic beliefs were unconscious and their origins mysterious to her.

As this vignette demonstrates, while pathogenic beliefs are children's inferences based on real experiences with caretakers, these inferences are not necessarily accurate. Children naturally construe their world from an egocentric point of view—a perspective in which children believe that the feelings and actions of those around them invariably have to do with them. This normal egocentricity leads children to blame themselves for things that have nothing to do with them. But even if irrational, such feelings of self-importance are also adaptive. Because of the life-or-death necessity of maintaining a secure attachment to parents, it is safer for children to assume that they can influence their caretaker than to assume that they can't.

Unfortunately, this exaggerated belief in our own power can also lead to all sorts of misunderstandings and false assumptions. A parent is unhappy? It's because we're too rambunctious. A parent easily loses his or her temper? It's because we're so provocative. An important benefit to this type of distortion, however, is that if it is our own fault, at least there is something we can try to do about it, namely, change ourselves.

Unconscious Sex

Many readers might well object that they are not aware of their pathogenic beliefs and therefore find it difficult to accept that their sexual fantasies and preferences arise as an attempt to overcome such beliefs. After all, sexual preferences feel natural. This problem people have with the idea that sexuality is psychologically complicated derives from the fact that the majority of our mental processes are unconscious, including the workings of sexual arousal.

You don't have to be a Freudian to believe in the power of the unconscious mind. Psychologists of all stripes have found that the unconscious mind has an enormous capacity to perceive psychological dangers and to fashion creative solutions rapidly and efficiently. Rather than being the cauldron of dark forces that Freud posited, the unconscious mind is now understood to be responsible for a great deal of information processing, implicit knowledge, and complex decision making. People are constantly scanning their environments, making judgments about others, arriving at decisions, and taking actions, all in the blink of an eye, and mostly without conscious intent or awareness.

A great deal of learning occurs at this deeper level, whether that learning involves physical or emotional skills. For example, we first learn to drive an automobile by consciously and deliberately making certain movements. Eventually, though, all of the complex perceptual and motor "decisions" that drivers make are made on an unconscious level. In fact, it's obvious that if we had to be aware of every judgment or decision we were making as we physically moved about in the world, we would be effectively paralyzed.

In a recent book, *Blink*, Malcolm Gladwell describes a myriad of split-second decisions and judgments that can only, in retrospect, be understood as the outcome of a complicated nonconscious process involving sorting, problem solving, and sophisticated inferences. Gladwell's examples of the positive uses of such intuitions include the capacity to tell if someone is lying, detecting art forgeries, diagnosing heart attacks, speed dating, tennis, and predicting divorce. The dark side of such subliminal intuition involves things like racial or ethnic stereotyping. Whether used for good or bad purposes, the speed and power of nonconscious decision making is incontrovertible.

Much of our emotional and social learning is also unconscious. Babies learn about the meaning of their mothers' moods, gestures, and intentions on a nonverbal level that is automatic and highly accurate. Research has shown—and parents intuitively understand—that even nonverbal infants and toddlers are exquisitely attuned to their caretakers' moods, gestures, and wishes. Such attunement and the learning that it informs do not ever have to be made conscious. The same processes occur in our adult interactions. When we engage someone in conversation we are "reading" that person continually, intuiting who they are and what they want, subliminally deciding how to connect with them and how not to. All of this happens below the radar of conscious awareness, and yet without it ordinary social intercourse would be impossible.

Not only would ordinary social life be impossible without the presence of nonconscious decision making, but a good deal of romantic life would be impossible as well. In one recent poll, 50 percent of respondents said that they believed in "love at first sight," and of these, 50 percent had directly experienced it. Such a romantic notion is impossible to comprehend without assuming that there is a level at which people "read" each other and intuit their potential compatibility.

Is it surprising, then, that the mind can and does navigate its way around and over psychological obstacles to achieve erotic outcomes just as rapidly? These outcomes might feel like impulses or reflexes, but like driving a car, they are actually the result of a complicated series of steps of which the conscious mind is unaware.

Decoding Sexual Fantasies

Armed with this model of the mind and the psychological dynamics of sexual arousal, male sexual fantasies and preferences need no longer be mysterious. All of the various forms of male sexuality reflect strategies to bypass or overcome the unconscious pathogenic beliefs that dampen erotic desire, beliefs involving feelings of worry, guilt, rejection, shame, loneliness, and helplessness. Further, if we can understand sexual behavior as an imaginary solution to underlying problems, then the distinction between the sexually conventional and bizarre breaks down. No matter how flamboyant or unusual the fantasy, its secret logic follows the same rules and can be divined and easily rendered comprehensible. The following brief examples will illustrate the wide range of phenomena explicable in this way.

Matt's central fantasy was to lie on the lap of a buxom woman and nurse like a baby while she masturbated him. Like many men, Matt seemed to be fixated on breasts. In his unconscious mind, breasts represented a woman who had a lot to give to a man and wanted to give it. Such a woman excited Matt because it negated his default belief that women were selfish, withholding, and resentful of their caretaker role. Matt had experienced his mother as chronically tired and self-centered, with little left over to give to her children. Matt's fantasy depiction of a voluptuous woman eager to feed and give him pleasure was, therefore, especially exciting.

Mick liked to be tied up and spanked by a strong woman. His underlying pathogenic belief involved the danger of feeling too powerful and potentially hurting women. This belief arose in a family context in which both parents, but particularly the mother, were depressive alcoholics. Mick felt burdened with feelings of responsibility and guilty about his feelings of contempt for his parents. In the bondage scenario, this belief was neatly and powerfully disconfirmed. The woman's strength signified that he couldn't hurt her. Because she was in control, he could let go of his need to be so. Because she was taking care of herself, he could as well. And because she was the aggressor, he didn't have to worry about his own aggression in any way. Mick could finally feel safe enough to become aroused.

Jerry was attracted to young, nubile women. He had a pathogenic belief that as women aged, they invariably became depressed, tired, and critical. Jerry's mother had become bitter after his father left her and she had stopped taking care of herself both physically and psychologically. He felt depressed when he was around her. In Jerry's mind, the "Lolita" figure represented a woman into whom he could plug himself and be recharged, a woman eager to please and easily pleased herself. She was, in his words, the "anti-mother" and, as a result, made it safe enough for him to get excited.

Ted got especially aroused watching a woman slowly undress for him. His underlying pathogenic belief was that women don't like male sexual attention and that men should feel guilty about thinking of women as primarily sexual objects and not as "whole people." Ted's mother hated men, beginning with her own abusive father and extending to her philandering husband. He remembered once overhearing her say that "the only good man was a dead man." She went out of her way to desexualize herself in dress and manner. In Ted's sexual life, however, when a woman stripped for him, the opposite was true. In this fantasy, the woman loved Ted's desire for her body, thus reassuring him that she wasn't hurt or offended.

Orrin became excited by the pornographic depiction of what are called "facials"—depictions of one or more men ejaculating on the face of a woman who is aroused by it. His underlying pathogenic belief involved an exaggerated worry and belief that all women tended to feel easily hurt and degraded by men. In his pornographic scenarios, women appeared to be the objects of extreme degradation, but instead of feeling degraded, they enjoyed it. Their enjoyment became a powerful marker in Orrin's mind for the reassuring fact that these women were not hurt.

Lloyd got a special sexual thrill from watching two women have sex. His underlying pathogenic belief was that women tend to be threatened by or disappointed in men, resulting in Lloyd feeling guilty and inadequate. When Lloyd was growing up, he felt that nothing he did was enough to make his mother happy. He inferred that he was somehow lacking as a boy and a person. So-called girl-on-girl sex was exciting because no men were directly involved. Watching two women, Lloyd could identify with one or both, safe from the guilt or performance anxiety that he might feel were he identifying with a man in the situation.

Pete became very aroused by the fantasy of having sex with several women at the same time. His pathogenic belief was that women don't have a lot to give to a man and, consequently, that his legitimate needs came to feel *greedy and overwhelming. His experience of his mother was of a woman chronically worried about money and status, as well as prone to hypochondria. In his fantasies of being with two women, Pete could get as much pleasure as he wanted without feeling guilty about depleting an individual woman with his sexual needs. Because he had half the worry, he could have double the pleasure.*

Cornell was especially aroused by high-heeled shoes on women. His pathogenic belief was that women are constitutionally weak and compliant. Growing up, Cornell saw his mother frequently exploited by men whom she idealized and to whom she surrendered her authority and autonomy. In Cornell's unconscious mind, the high-heeled shoe represented strength. It was phallic, sharp, and powerful. A woman in such shoes gratified his wish that women be strong and thus mitigated his guilt and responsibility.

Anthony, a gay man, preferred to be a "bottom" during sex. He had the pathogenic belief that he had little to offer a man. He grew up with a harshly critical father and absent mother. Such an environment destroyed Anthony's self-esteem. The excitement he derived from being the receptive partner in sex was the result of the reassurance that because his partner was calling the shots, he would therefore be completely satisfied. Freed of his worry about pleasing his partner, Anthony then felt safe enough to get aroused.

Harold was a "top" in the local gay community. He had the pathogenic belief that in relationships there was always a danger of being rendered helpless, a belief that had arisen in response to his treatment by a terrifying and abusive father. He reported frequent beatings and terrifying rages fuelled by his father's alcoholism. Only when he was completely in charge of a sexual interaction could he felt safe enough to become excited.

These are only thumbnail vignettes, of course, but they illustrate the point that the superficial meaning or intention of a sexual fantasy or preference is often contradicted by its deeper motivation. The meaning of sex is often marked by opposites. Thus, while Mick liked to be dominated so as to not feel guilty and responsible, we will encounter other men who like to dominate in order to transcend feelings of helplessness. The exhibitionist is aroused because he momentarily overcomes shame and rejection. The male voyeur loves to "watch" so as to not feel watched himself.

Once we accept that sexual predilections are actually psychological strategies to solve problems and not biological or moral deviations, we can stop feeling ashamed of them. Sexual fantasies become perfectly understandable, and people are often relieved to find that they may well mean the opposite of what they appear to mean. Analyzing sexual desires from the inside out immediately renders them sensible. We need to understand them as solutions rather than as dangerous secrets.

Before we explore the vicissitudes of male sexuality, however, we must take up this question: Why do men have differing pathogenic beliefs than women do, and how did they develop different sexual techniques for overcoming them?

What's Different about Male Sexuality and Why?

WHILE BOTH MEN AND WOMEN have unconscious minds, the subterranean paths they take to sexual pleasure are different. This difference begins in childhood. Boys and girls start out with a similar problem, namely, from the absolute dependence of infancy, how do children grow up and become independent of their caretakers while at the same time remaining connected to them? And since in our culture the primary caretakers of the young are usually women, the more precise question is: how do children separate from women—mothers—and yet still maintain a loving relationship with them?

This is a universal problem, and yet it takes a different form for boys and girls. While both genders have to separate from their mothers, boys have the additional task of identifying with an entirely different gender. Boys not only have to become individuals apart from their mothers but masculine ones as well. Girls have to establish their difference from their mothers but not from their mothers' gender. In this one crucial sense, the developmental task for boys is more complicated than it is for girls.

Reinforced by certain gender stereotypes in our culture, boys often accomplish this twofold task of leaving the nest and becoming masculine by making masculinity into the negation or rejection of femininity. The result is that their separation process tends to take on a harsher and more rigid quality than that of girls. For boys, growing up does not simply mean becoming masculine, but becoming *not* feminine. Dependency becomes equated with being like a girl and, as a result, has to be forcefully rejected. The internal push to individuate meets the external pull of gender socialization to create a hyper-autonomous boy actively pushing away all vestiges of the femininity originally embodied in his first and primary object of attachment—his mother.

This need to deny the gender of the mother more actively puts a special twist on the developmental process of boys in three important ways. First, as boys push away from their mothers, they are vulnerable to feelings of guilt and worry about hurting and therefore jeopardizing their connections with the very caretakers they love and need the most. More than girls, boys have to reject symbolically someone they need and about whose welfare they care and worry deeply. The second consequence of the gender rigidity involved in masculine development is that boys have more to lose than girls by closeness to the mother and, later, to others. Emotional intimacy always involves some measure of identification—a sense of being *like* the object of affection. But since boys already have had to work harder than girls to feel like separate people, the threat to this separateness posed by intimacy is correspondingly greater as well. And the third consequence of the special connection in boys between masculinity and separation is a propensity to feel emotionally disconnected. If guilt and longings for closeness to the mother are especially threatening to boys in their quest for masculinity, then donning the emotional armor of stoicism and self-sufficiency is a natural solution, but one for which boys pay a high emotional price.

We see this later in the experience of men defensively resisting too much intimacy with women. Caught between their desire for closeness and fears of losing their sense of separateness and masculinity, such men establish ambivalent relationships with women. One male patient of mine told me that the two situations in which he could be safely close to his wife were when they were driving in a car or watching television together. In both situations, he experienced the optimal combination of connection and separation, together but not facing each other in a way that invited more (to him) fusion. He liked to quote Antoine de Saint Exupéry to me, who said, "Love does not consist in gazing at each other, but in looking together in the same direction." His wife, who sought out more direct contact with him, referred to Saint Exupéry as "that French moron."

Another patient of mine expressed his characteristically male ambivalence about closeness to women by a common male habit in the bedroom, namely, after sex he would immediately withdraw and roll over and away from his partner. During lovemaking, he was intensely present, but the moment it was over he had to detach himself from his lover's body and psyche. Like many men, he felt vulnerable to and easily engulfed by women if he wasn't hard and aroused.

The contradictions in which masculinity is grounded inevitably find their way into the bedroom. The special developmental need not only to leave the mother but to reject her femininity casts shadows on male development, the shadows of guilt, an exaggerated fear of closeness, and emotional isolation. And it is within this darkness that male sexual fantasies and preferences are born.

Optimally, fathers help their boys with these dilemmas by providing positive role models and paternal encouragement for their sons' budding masculinity. Boys want to have close relationships with fathers who are proud of their own masculinity and motivated to support that of their sons. Unfortunately, such optimal conditions are rare. Fathers in our culture are often perceived as absent, emotionally or physically, and are frequently seen as in conflict with their wives. Healthy masculine role models are hard to come by. Too often, boys are left alone to navigate the complicated currents of their relationships with their mothers and, by extension, other women.

These particular tensions in male development leave boys vulnerable to a special type of guilt about being masculine. In our culture, masculinity is often founded on a negation of the femininity represented by the mother. Boys grow up with the belief, however irrational, that one of the most basic ways they can potentially hurt women is by simply being male. Masculinity itself—and the character traits associated with it such as assertiveness and strength—is experienced by the boy as inherently in conflict with the world of women, a world perceived as potentially opposed to or hurt by the boy's development.

It makes sense that boys might worry that their masculinity could hurt their mothers. After all, our culture encourages boys to not only prize their own gender but to devalue the opposite one. And, as we've seen, boys are also working internally to resolve the problem of separating from their mothers by exaggerating the specialness of their masculine difference.

Despite the cultural encouragement to do so, boys don't inherently want to reject or devalue their mothers to become masculine. Like all children they love their mothers and want them to be healthy and happy. The belief that masculinity necessarily hurts women is, therefore, often a pathogenic belief. At their deepest level, boys want their mothers to be happy not only with their own gender but their own lives. Such basic wishes are not simply loving but also reflective of boys' need for reassurance that their own growth and pleasure in their masculine difference will not hurt their beloved caretakers. Unfortunately, boys often grow up with the false and painful belief that their separation has hurt their mothers or that their own pride in being masculine is the object of maternal envy. The resulting guilt can cause a range of problems: it can force some boys to play down their difference, suppress their pleasure, or mute their pride in their masculinity. Or as we'll see, it can make boys exaggerate their masculinity to dramatically drown out the voices of worry and regret.

One patient I treated grew up struggling with the fear that by being too much of a traditional boy he would make his mother more depressed than she already was. When he entered puberty he gave up all competitive sports and became extremely shy and withdrawn around girls. Another patient with a similar type of guilt about his masculinity developed a childhood symptom in which he felt a chronic sense of irritation in and around his penis, despite the complete absence of any physical grounds for this sensation. The only way he found relief was by pushing his penis partway back up into his inguinal canal where it then felt snug and secure. In both cases, the boys developed symptoms as a results of their pathogenic guilt about hurting their mothers with their phallic masculinity.

Mothers often add to their sons' difficulties in several ways. They may, in reality, envy and resent the fact that their sons are growing up, leaving their sphere of influence and laying claim to privileges from which some mothers may feel excluded. The caricature of the Jewish mother making her son feel guilty taps into this reality ("you never call, you never write"). Moreover, many of these mothers may, in reality, be unhappy with their lot in life, creating the conditions under which their sons might naturally feel guilty about the process of becoming separate, independent, and masculine.

It is natural to worry about someone you love and on whom you depend. Children are highly attuned to the moods of their mothers and are liable to take responsibility for either causing or fixing these moods. Therefore, to the extent that mothers are dissatisfied about aspects of their lives unrelated to their sons, their sons will still likely infer that it has something to do with them, with what they feel or want, including their feelings about their masculinity.

The effects of such guilt and worry are varied and not limited to sex. One male patient of mine tended to act very needy with women because of a subliminal assumption that his independence would make women feel useless. Another patient found that he frequently became friends and not lovers with women. He had the unconscious belief that being sexually assertive would offend the opposite sex. Another patient liked to frequent prostitutes because by virtue of their job and the cash transaction involved, he could imagine that these women welcomed his masculine sexual urges and so weren't burdened by them. So-called normal women, he believed, would feel repelled by aggressive displays of male desire. In still another, more extreme, case, a patient of mine liked to wear women's panties. Upon exploration it emerged that he was unconsciously and symbolically reassuring women—originally his mother—that he didn't really feel pride about being a man.

Finally, I have seen a host of men who seem to deal with their guilt about hurting women by becoming caricatures of masculinity, disconnecting to such a degree that they aren't even consciously aware of women's feelings, much less feel responsible for them. It is the men who employ this solution who are perceived and experienced by women as "typical" men, seeking sex for its own sake, selfishly taking what they want, indifferent to the emotional needs of their partners. For these men, the macho ideal of masculinity is emptied not only of normal needs and longings for the opposite sex, but of all capacity for empathy, guilt, and worry as well. One patient of mine who grew up feeling chronically emasculated by a critical mother he could never satisfy used to only refer to women as "bitches." His relationships were superficial, primarily sexual, and short-lived. Upon exploration it became clear that he was terrified that in a real intimate relationship he would come to feel so sucked into his partner's feelings that he would end up feeling overwhelmingly helpless and guilty. His primary problem was his deep sense of inadequacy about satisfying women and an equally deep feeling of responsibility for doing just that. His solution was to enact a role that negated both dangers.

Girls have their own conflicts over growing up and becoming independent that are every bit as complex as those of boys. Girls also have to separate from their mothers and suffer their own significant share of guilt and anxiety about this process. However, because girls don't have to renounce— to *dis*identify with—the gender of their mothers and therefore don't have to pull away as forcefully as boys, they can remain embedded in the mother-child relationship longer and more deeply.

Developmental research, reinforced by my own clinical experience, tells us that mothers see themselves in their daughters more than their sons, often projecting their unrealized ambitions and fears onto their daughters, who then became burdened with a special type of responsibility. As Nancy Friday showed in her popular book *My Mother, My Self,* many women spend their entire lives consciously or unconsciously close to their mothers, often worrying about and trying to please them despite conscious intentions to do otherwise. The benefits of this connection are that girls don't have to cut off their empathy and feelings as much as boys do; the costs, however, are that girls often feel inordinately guilty about having more success in their work and love lives than their mothers.

The sexual consequence of this particular type of guilt in girls is that they tend to inhibit their own active sexual desires out of a belief that they don't deserve to have more success and pleasure in this realm than their mothers. For many women, enjoying a carefree and intensely pleasurable sex life unconsciously feels like dancing on their mothers' graves. For girls, the "crime" is to be a sexually independent and assertive person; for boys, the "crime" is to be a masculine one.

A woman patient recently confessed that when she was having great sex, she sometimes thought of her mother living in a loveless marriage, and her excitement would begin to wane. Other female patients have talked about how their mothers were often highly ambivalent about their daughters' sexuality, alternately voyeuristic and prohibitive. As my patients explored these memories, they remembered sensing that underlying both the vicarious excitement and punitive restrictions lay not only objective worries about such things as disease and pregnancy but also their mothers' envy of their daughters' sexual exuberance, intensity, and success. Such envy—whether real or imagined—fueled the guilt that led to later sexual inhibitions.

One patient of mine who was especially shut down sexually told me that when she was first dating in high school, she would come home and stay up late regaling her mother about her dates, usually about the ineptitude of her boyfriends. The patient's father was an invalid and her mother was his sole caretaker. By including her mother in her romantic life, my patient was not only providing vicarious excitement to her overburdened and lonely mother, but unconscious reassurance that the daughter was not going to be more successful than the mother when it came to love and sex. When it came to starting her own family, the patient felt troubled by persistent feelings of guilt and disloyalty, which eventually led to her sexual inhibitions.

In addition, early experiences with fathers who are either remote or domineering accentuate the type of guilt that leads to later sexual repression in girls. Such fathers are often experienced as weak and, in girls' imaginations, rendered so by something bad in the daughters. A common fantasy among women is that if they were to really let go of all sexual inhibitions and express their sexual passion fully, men, like their fathers, would feel threatened and then defensively react by abandoning or humiliating them. A corollary fear for many women is that their sexual appeal is so powerful that men will lose control of their own sexual impulses and imperil the women with some form of violent sexual response. When men appear to lack impulse control, women perceive them not only as frightening but as weak. The result is that women expect to be punished for either intimidating men or making them lose control.

In response to this danger, women often keep the full measure of their sexual passion under control, or enact, in fantasy or reality, sexual scenarios in which men are maintained as strong and in control. Domination fantasies surely fall under this rubric—the "top" or dominator, after all, cannot be hurt or overwhelmed by the submissive or helpless "bottom." I saw these dynamics clearly in my work with a patient whom I call Jan.

Jan, was a feminist academic who was widely regarded as someone who "didn't take any shit," particularly from men. She consulted me because she was unhappy in her present relationship with a man whom she described as too "wimpy" and "passive." She felt ambivalent, however, because he was also quite caring toward her, a quality that she valued highly. Jan described a relationship pattern that is not uncommon among my women patients. She wanted her boyfriend to be stronger so she didn't have to feel responsible for everything. When he deferred too much, Jan would feel burdened and alone. Why did she always have to direct their lives? she complained. Why couldn't he take charge more? Jan would respond to her boyfriend's self-effacement by becoming angry and critical, which would make him even more timid, which would then make her feel more guilty, which would then lead her to be more critical, and so on. If he acted strong, on the other hand, Jan would privately feel relief but would test his ability to "handle" her by first reacting in a bitchy way. Unfortunately, her boyfriend would often fail the test by capitulating, thus starting the process all over again.

At some point in her work with me, Jan confessed that she had a sexual fantasy that she used to masturbate and to have an orgasm while having sex with her boyfriend. Although it emerged over the course of several weeks, I have condensed her account into the following narrative:

I sometimes imagine that I'm sitting in my office, working diligently at my computer. It's late and the building is empty. Suddenly my door opens and a custodian enters, saying that he needs to empty the waste-basket, which happens to be under my desk. I'm curt with him and tell him to hurry up. I notice that he's quite big and well-muscled under his uniform. As he reaches under my desk for the wastebasket, he suddenly runs his hand up my leg, under my skirt, and roughly squeezes my cunt. I start to resist. He grabs my hands, holds them together over my head with one hand, and with the other hand lifts me onto my desk, spreads my legs, and rips off my panties. He tells me that he's wanted to fuck me for a long time. His cock is huge. His whole body is massive. He's so strong that I can't move. He squeezes my tits hard. The thing is, while he's fucking me, he isn't even looking at me. Sometimes the scenario involves him grabbing my head and fucking my mouth. Other times, it's my ass. But it's as if he has to not only have a hard prick, he has to be a prick as a person. He has to not give a shit about my pleasure but instead just use my body as something to fuck and something to give him pleasure. He's exactly the kind of asshole that I've hated my whole life, and yet this fantasy gets me so hot that I can reach orgasm with it in minutes.

The key ingredients in the story are that the man is huge and utterly indifferent, and Jan is helpless. She is not an active sexual agent but a passive victim. And she's not hurting anyone. In the fantasy, Jan is not responsible for the man in any way—in fact, he's just a "prick" and she doesn't have to be aware of his needs, much less take care of them. Jan was relieved to realize that her feminist attitudes did not cover up a secret wish to be weak, but that instead her fantasies all involved her guilt about having any type of aggressive sexual desire or being too strong, and about her irrational need to protect men.

Jan's fear of experiencing unbridled sexual excitement had its origins in family dynamics familiar to many women's. Her mother was a hard-working woman, combining part-time substitute teaching with full-time caretaking for her three children. On an emotional level, however, Jan also experienced her as grim and martyred. Jan's father was an intermittently successful real estate agent whose moods fluctuated with his income. He could be charming one week and a bully the next. Jan remembered walking on eggshells around him, never knowing what was going to set him off. This volatility got worse as Jan entered adolescence and became more independent in thought and deed.

Jan experienced both her parents as weak in different ways, but ways that similarly left a deep mark on her sexual life. She came to feel sorry for her mother and secretly disdainful of and disappointed in her father. She developed the pathogenic belief that she wasn't supposed to have more pleasure—of any kind—than her mother and that openly demanding or needing too much from a man would be dangerous.

Girls and boys, then, grow up navigating around different dangers associated with sexual arousal. Daughters learn to put a lid on their sexuality; sons on their masculinity.

Survivor Guilt

A powerful example of how a universal conflict becomes overlaid with gender-specific meanings can be found in the experience of survivor guilt. Originally intended to describe the feelings observed in survivors of traumas such as the Holocaust (for example, that they didn't deserve to live while others had died), survivor guilt is often used now by psychologists to describe the belief that life in general is a zero-sum game—the more I get, the less there is for you.

Many children of both sexes grow up with the unconscious belief that they're not supposed to have more of the good things in life than their mothers, good things like being happy in work or love, having pleasure, or being strong. In these cases, survivor guilt is based on a belief that the child's gain is the mother's loss, that the child hurts the mother simply by being successful.

Survivor guilt is all around us. Who hasn't felt bad about having more than others or leaving others behind? Who hasn't felt a whisper of fraudulence about success because of the guilty sense that they are overreaching? Many people, in fact, who cannot easily tolerate success because of survivor guilt unconsciously arrange to fail. How often do we read about an athlete who escapes the ghetto to achieve success only to self-destruct? Certainly people who get promotions sometimes become depressed rather than excited. For many people, success is a crime and invites punishment.

While survivor guilt is important in the psyches of both men and women, it often has a unique quality in men, a quality already referred to in prior descriptions of the special forms taken by male guilt. Many of my male patients grew up inferring that their mothers felt victimized by men and, as a result, became uncomfortable themselves about feeling or acting too masculine around women. Their guilt about separation and success was often exaggerated by the belief that not only were they leaving their mothers by growing up, but also they were leaving their mothers behind by excluding them from the special pleasures and triumphs associated with masculinity. As adults, these men often came to feel overly responsible for the women with whom they were involved, guilty about being too selfish— including sexually selfish—and then resentful about such obligations. Often, such men came to feel inordinately sensitive to any hint of displeasure in women, privately worried that it was their fault, and often felt like "bad guys" as a result.

As mentioned earlier, another reaction that boys often have to the special nature of their survivor guilt is to become hypermasculine. Following the logic of the Shakespearean heroine who, in denying her love, did "protest too much," men sometimes deny their survivor guilt by acting as if women and their feelings don't matter to them at all. Their unconscious logic is: "I am so different from women, so separate from them, that their feelings can't affect me." The guilt is present in the very force of its denial.

Sexual Ruthlessness

After decades of studying the role of guilt in producing gender differences in sexual desire, I have been impressed with the frequency with which both sexes, but particularly men, feel guilty about being selfish. When it comes to the problems linked to pathogenic beliefs to which men seek sexual solutions, one of the most important involves guilt about what I call the *ruthless* dimension of sexual excitement.

A British psychoanalyst, D. W. Winnicott, used the term *ruthless* to describe the normal phase of early child development in which the child uses the mother as if she were a thing, taking for granted that the mother will not be hurt by and will endure the child's separation. When applied to sexual feelings, the concept of ruthlessness has a similar meaning; it refers to the fact that sexual excitement requires that we momentarily become selfish and turn away from concerns about the other's pleasure to surrender to our own, that we momentarily stop worrying about hurting or rejecting the other person. Ruthlessness refers to the capacity to "use" another person without concern that the other will feel used. It is a normal and necessary part of healthy sexual desire.

When I refer to "using" another person, I am not talking about actually disregarding the feelings of the other but about a quality of relatedness in which the other person is experienced as not needing to be taken care of and thus can be taken for granted. "Using" the other, then, means that one is not obligated to worry about his or her pleasure and can surrender to one's own selfish excitement without guilt or burdensome feelings of responsibility. One patient told me that when he had to be too aware of doing the "right thing" during sex, he couldn't really let go and fully enjoy himself. He told me that in his current sexual relationship, he and his partner could just "fuck our brains out" with abandon and without undue concern about whether or not the other was having fun. Another patient told me that sexual excitement to her felt like a "wave crashing against the shore." The "shore" was sturdy, firm, and unyielding. She didn't want to worry if the shore could take it.

I am not arguing that selfishness should be a sexual ideal; at its best, sexual pleasure is deeply entwined with a sensitivity to the feelings of our partner and a pleasurable desire to give him or her pleasure. Love is sexy, and sex enhances love. However, in my clinical experience, sexual excitement most often breaks down under the weight of worry and guilt precisely because of conflicts over the selfish dimension of desire, conflicts that become worse, not better, with the increasing familiarity and intimacy of long-term relationships. Simply put, people feel guilty about being ruthless, about being too selfish, and they imagine that such an attitude hurts or neglects others.

When people feel guilty about being ruthless, the guilt can manifest itself in many different ways. They can worry that the other person will be hurt. They can worry that the person will be angry, as if he or she would be offended by any whiff of selfishness. Several men I've treated feel that they can only ask their partners for fellatio *after* satisfying them with cunnilingus. Or they can worry that the other person will be indifferent or rejecting. For example, one man I saw couldn't ask for anything too "dirty" from a woman in bed because of his fears that she would inevitably be disgusted. Few people would describe these feelings as guilt, and yet in all of these scenarios, guilt is the primary culprit because each of them is, in their own way, a punishment fantasy. The logic goes: "I'm not supposed to be self-assertive and take what I want because I will hurt or offend the other person. If I do, I'll be punished by that person's pain, anger, or rejection." Crime and punishment: the crime is being ruthless; ruthlessness evokes guilt, and guilt leads to a real or imagined punishment in the form of some kind of painful outcome.

The normal ruthlessness inherent in healthy sexual excitement becomes problematic for men in somewhat different ways than it does for women. Men in our culture already have guilt-based conflicts about distancing themselves from too much involvement with women's inner lives;

after all, one of the contradictions within masculinity itself lies in the apparent necessity of just such a denial. As we've seen, the need to reject femininity regularly threatens men with special feelings of guilt and fears of intimacy. In this context, empathy in relationships is itself especially dangerous for men because it involves temporarily feeling what women are feeling. Empathy involves seeing the world from the other's point of view, a task made difficult in a male psyche constructed to keep its distance from women.

On the basis of this observation, it might be argued that ruthlessness is the natural state for men. Shouldn't their conflict about empathy make sexual ruthlessness easier and less problematic for men? If healthy sexuality requires the capacity to *not* worry about the other's welfare, don't men have a natural advantage over women when it comes to ruthlessness? The answer is no. Men are *not* more ruthless than women; in fact, they have special difficulties with ruthlessness that women don't have.

We must remember that the development of normal masculinity carries with it an unhealthy burden of guilt about hurting women. But when men react to this burden by objectifying or pushing women away, this is not true healthy sexual ruthlessness at all. Sexual ruthlessness—the *healthy* capacity to be selfish and not overly attuned to one's partner—becomes confused with the *unhealthy* need to rigidly avoid intimate emotional connections. The guilt and fear connected to the latter need gets confused by both men and women with the guilt and fear about exercising healthy ruthlessness. As a result, men too often carry a special burden of guilt about hurting women, and women too often see men as deserving that burden. Neither gender can accurately see that the real problem men have is not too much ruthlessness but too little!

Male anxieties about emotional closeness are not the same as the healthy exercise of sexual selfishness. The guilty need in men to push women away and the resulting fearful need to avoid intimacy is not the same as healthy sexual ruthlessness. In fact, men suffer from a surplus of the former and a deficit in the latter. Men are actually too guilty about being truly selfish in bed with women, not too free about it. They suffer from being overly worried about hurting or failing to satisfy women, not being overly indifferent to them.

But because of the confusion between the two, it is difficult for both sexes to accept the argument that men suffer from a diminished—not exaggerated—capacity to be sexually selfish. In fact, men unreasonably inhibit their ruthlessness. Such a claim contradicts the common belief that male sexuality is often openly selfish and that it is women who have a more difficult time being selfish and assertive in their erotic lives. However, it is crucial to remember that the fact that men *appear* to be sexually selfish does not mean that they *feel* that way. Ruthlessness is entirely subjective. Thus, it behooves all of us to peer behind the surface of male behavior and investigate what men are actually feeling.

For example, it is common in heterosexual couples for women to complain that their male partners are selfish and emotionally unavailable. And, in fact, as we've seen, it is undeniable that men tend to be more emotionally disconnected than women, and often resentful of the latter's pleas for engagement. Such resentment can appear quite selfish. However, this is not ruthlessness. The real reasons that these men reject their partners' pleas for empathy and connection are (1) that because of their chronic guilt about their masculinity and the resulting exaggerated responsibility they feel for women, men already chronically feel (rightly or wrongly) that they are supposed to sacrifice their own needs for those of their partners, and therefore experience a demand for empathy as a demand for *more* self-abnegation and sacrifice, and (2) that they unconsciously equate intimacy—and their own desire for it—with a weakening of their masculine boundaries.

Many men are actually highly sensitive to evidence that their partners are unhappy or unsatisfied, feeling that the satisfaction of women, like that of their mothers, is their responsibility and yet almost impossible to achieve. This is the legacy of their guilt about their masculinity. The price they pay for these feelings of guilt and responsibility is a dampening of sexual excitement. For example, men often correctly perceive that their female partners need them to remain in close emotional contact during sex, but they experience this need as an obligation, one that inhibits them from surrendering to their own internal sensations. *The reason that a woman's need becomes the man's obligation is because of the unconscious belief that he is supposed to satisfy a woman's needs.* Caught between feeling resentful that they have to suppress their own needs to make women happy, and feeling guilty about their chronic failure to do so, men are often unable to pursue sexual pleasure with even a momentary disregard for their partners. Healthy ruthlessness threatens to inflame the underlying guilt at the foundation of masculinity. Guilty about their wish to be more ruthless, such men will often shut down. Such disengagement will then be experienced by their partners as selfish.

Emotional detachment in men during and after sex is experienced by women as selfish and uncaring when, in fact, it is the end product of a conflict between healthy wishes to be ruthless and inordinate feelings of responsibility to make women happy.

My patient Loren was a psychotherapist who sought help for sexual problems in his marriage. His wife complained that Loren was utterly detached and mechanical during sex. She complained that he selfishly sought his own satisfaction and was oblivious to her needs. Loren complained to me that his wife was like "all women . . . always ragging on men about something." This tough way of talking was belied by Loren's internal experience in which he was highly attuned to and aware of every nuance of his wife's demeanor and mood. The problem, Loren eventually revealed, was that he had failed to perform sexually with his wife on several prior occasions and the resulting shame he felt was devastating to him. He felt that the only way he could stay hard was to focus inward on some pornographic fantasy until he was confident he could successfully maintain his potency.

Ultimately, Loren's difficulty maintaining his erections during sex with his wife had to do with his experience of her as critical and readily dissatisfied. In order to perform, then, Loren had to disconnect from her by focusing entirely on someone else. His wife understandably experienced him as selfish and disconnected; the truth of the matter was that Loren was unable to *not* care sufficiently about his wife's welfare to successfully surrender to his own sensations and desires while remaining in contact with her. His problem was not that he was too ruthless but not ruthless enough.

Guilt is not the only pathogenic belief and feeling around which men and women differ. Boys and girls also grow up feeling different degrees of isolation and loneliness. Because boys have to establish their independence and gender identity with more force than do girls, they risk feeling more emotionally cut off. Much has been written about the high price that boys pay for the apparent benefits of being inducted into masculine social roles in our society. The sacrifice of friendships with girls, the prominence of teasing and competition in male relationships, the prohibitions about revealing feelings, the association of dependence with weakness—all are isolation-producing consequences of the unfortunate fact that masculinity is grounded in the negation of femininity. The result is that the boy and the man he will later become struggles with a special type of loneliness.

Girls are certainly often lonely, but, as expert researchers into the origins of feminine development have argued, since the separation process of girls is less rigid and reactive than that of boys, they experience relationships and intimacy as safer. Girls remain more connected to their mothers, related to others, and comfortable with intimacy than do boys.

A Further View from the Couch:
Two Cases, Two Worlds

In the real world, these issues are complicated. When we descend from the heights of theory to the muddy ground on which real men and women walk, gender differences are neither as stark nor as clear as we would like. Nevertheless, it is to the messy interior lives of two real people that we now turn.

The Case of Jim

When Jim first consulted me, he reminded me of a mountain man. He wasn't exactly rugged—he had spent his professional life in offices—but he had an air of earthy self-reliance about him. He had a full head of blond hair and usually wore jeans and a flannel shirt to our sessions. His manner was reserved and stoic. Though he was superficially friendly, Jim's warmth seemed at first a bit studied. He would act like someone who was relaxed and playful, often giving me a big bear hug upon entering our sessions, and yet I often sensed considerable tension underneath. It was as if Jim was trying to convince himself and others that he was someone he was not. In fact, Jim's everyday life felt disconnected, even to him. He rarely had much real fun but instead felt life to be a series of unfinished tasks that he felt obliged to complete. He was retired but complained that he felt like a workaholic.

Jim was having problems in his marriage. He had married a woman of German descent, tall, blond, and athletic, whom he experienced as both strong and "high-maintenance." She tended to be critical and reactive to any signs of rejection from Jim, and he often felt that he had to "manage" her to stay out of trouble. He pictured his wife like a rose bush, beautiful but prickly. Jim often daydreamed about other women. In his fantasies, he liked them young and lean. Given our culture's idealization of youth and thinness, there was nothing unusual about Jim's sexual preference except for the fact that Jim was especially fixated on breasts.

He loved breasts. He loved to look at them, imagine them, touch them, and suck them. While another man would also notice a woman's derriere, Jim would only notice her breasts. For example, he might describe a woman he found attractive by saying, "She was quite pretty . . . nice body . . . oh, and really nice breasts." His first therapist told him that he had not gotten enough love from his mother and that his breast fixation represented a secret wish for a woman to demonstrate her love through nursing him. His second therapist told him that he was afraid of intimacy with a real and complete woman and psychically reduced women to breasts to feel safe. Neither interpretation made much sense to Jim.

Jim had little doubt, though, about the truth that he was deprived by his mother. He described her as a bitter woman who was abandoned by his father when Jim was twelve. His few memories of his early life were of his parents fighting and, later, of his grim mother working hard to support him and his two siblings. Jim's mother often seemed strained and unavailable, leading him to feel guilty about wanting too much attention or caretaking from her. Unfortunately, his father was even worse, at first spending their occasional weekends together complaining about Jim's mother, and eventually abandoning the family altogether. If breasts represented love, Jim's fixation on them was certainly understandable.

However, his former therapists' interpretations weren't helpful because they failed to grasp the real issue: Jim was overwhelmed with guilt. In Jim's psyche, breasts represented a woman who had a lot to give to a man and who, moreover, would be happy giving it to him. The real problem with feeling deprived as a child was that Jim grew up with the false and painful idea that women didn't like making men happy, that they were too preoccupied to be empathic, and that he didn't deserve their attention anyway. As long as he felt guilty about wanting something that he didn't deserve, and wanting too much of it, Jim couldn't possibly get turned on. His fantasy about sucking and playing with breasts precisely counteracted these ideas about women and made it safe enough for him to get aroused. In his mind, breasts were the clearest symbol of a woman's willingness to give to him. Momentarily freed from this guilt by his breast fantasy, Jim was free to experience his excitement.

When I offered this explanation to Jim, he instantly "got it" and talked to me about how rare it was for any woman in his life to go out of her way to help or comfort him and that when one did—for example, his housekeeper or physician—he felt enormously moved by and attracted to that woman. A breast was simply a marker for Jim's forbidden dream of mutuality.

Breasts, then, and the generous empathic woman that they represented, promised Jim relief from the strain of his everyday life. And if attractive breasts were attached to a woman who was also young and lithe, then all the better for Jim. A woman's unblemished and exuberant youth was like an energy cell in Jim's mind, something into which he could plug himself and escape an inner world populated by lonely, deprived boys and tired, bitter women.

Jim and I explored the underlying dynamics of his breast fixation for many months. The insights it generated about the difficulties he had in other parts of his life were useful to him. He came to understand how disconnected he really was and that many of his social interactions suffered as a result. Further, Jim came to see that he had probably married a woman who was difficult to please because he secretly believed that he didn't deserve love that came easily to him. Armed with these insights, Jim began to experiment with trying less hard when he was with people, but to tell more of his friends about his interior struggles and the grim way that he often experienced life. As a result, his friends became more solicitous of Jim and sought him out more. He began to confront his wife about her reactivity and judgmental attitude, which resulted in them seeking out couples therapy. However, while the underlying disturbances in Jim's capacity for mutuality changed, his breast fetish remained constant.

Although Jim used an idiosyncratic fantasy of breasts to counteract his sense of internal frustration, the character type that underlay his frustration is similar to that of many men. While the official canon of psychiatric diagnosis would say that he had an obsessive-compulsive or avoidant personality, when it came right down to it, Jim was a typical man in many respects. On an unconscious level he felt disconnected and guilty, burdened with the responsibility for satisfying women who ultimately couldn't be satisfied, a sensibility that I often see in my male patients.

The Case of Deborah

Deborah's story captures many of these psychological and social sensitivities and reactions particular to women. In her late thirties, Deborah began seeing me for help with a lifelong problem with depression. She was a beautiful woman who thought she was ugly, a slim woman with a good figure who thought she was fat, and a very bright woman who thought she was stupid. She had had a series of highly sexual relationships that, she said, were satisfying to her primarily because they were satisfying to her partner. In fact, Deborah admitted, her most intense sexual pleasure derived primarily from looking at her partner's face during sex, especially when he had an orgasm.

Deborah rarely initiated sex but readily participated when her partner made the first move. Deborah was afraid of letting go. She didn't know why, but she had the fantasy that if she lost control of her sexual feelings, it would lead to some unknown catastrophe. She liked to watch a man lose control of his feelings, but kept hers under wraps. Surrendering to her own internal erotic sensations without maintaining constant contact with her boyfriend was threatening to her.

Understanding Deborah's background gave us most of the clues necessary to decode her erotic life. Her father was expressive and charismatic but also physically explosive and abusive toward his children. Deborah remembers multiple scenes at the dinner table in which something she said, or the way she said it, or the look on her face, would provoke her father into a frenzy and would result in a beating. She had many memories of her father chasing her around the house, of locking herself in the bathroom or hiding in a closet, intermingled with memories of her father's public charm and popularity and her mother's utter passivity when it came to her husband's emotional volatility. Deborah developed the pathogenic belief that when it came to men, she was either repulsive or provocative.

Deborah had no memories of having had any inappropriate sexual contact with her father. However, her father's frequent losses of control, even if they involved his temper and not his sexuality, left a mark on Deborah in the form of her fear of men unpredictably losing control. This loss of control was not only frightening to her as a child, but also made her father and men in general seem weak and pathetic. Deborah had developed a burdensome sense of omnipotence based on a pathogenic belief that she caused her father's angry outbursts, that she had the power to provoke him to lose control, and as a result, she had to continually monitor and control herself with men. She also felt guilty about her capacity to render men pathetic. Not only did she feel rejected and disparaged by her father, leading to a chronic insecurity about her desirability in a man's eyes, but she also feared that if she wasn't careful, she could weaken a man by making him lose control.

When Deborah was having sex with a man, she liked to watch him lose control because in those moments the man's excitement seemed to be under her control and was animated by his intense desire for her. Her arousal was based on pleasing the man and giving him something he valued. In the process, however, she lost a sense of her own sexual agency. There were times during sex, Deborah told me, that she wasn't sure that she was doing what she wanted or simply complying with her boyfriend's desire. She couldn't comfortably initiate sex for herself because of her fear that her boyfriend would, like her father, reject her.

Deborah's mother frequently communicated her disappointment about various aspects of her daughter's appearance and behavior. Deborah was told that she was too fat, that her hairstyle was unattractive, and her features too coarse and homely. Deborah told me that her mother still disparaged her appearance, even as an adult. For example, her mother once came to the small Midwest town in which Deborah was then living and they went out to lunch with Deborah's friend Katy. Her mother spent the lunch admiring Katy's hair, her hands, and her complexion, frequently mentioning in a sweet but forlorn voice that she wished that Deborah looked more like her friend.

In addition, Deborah's experience and perception was that her mother was completely asexual, or even antisexual. Her mother confided in Deborah that she herself didn't really like sex and that the pain of intercourse with Deborah's father had been so bad that she went to a doctor to have her vagina dilated, a procedure that was often done in the 1940s as a treatment for what was then called "vaginismus." Deborah recovered a powerful memory from her late adolescence in which much of this dynamic between her and her mother was condensed. Deborah was seventeen and came home after a date on which she had just had sex for the first time. Her mother was up late, waiting for her. Deborah pulled up a chair and they started talking. Suddenly, her mother said, out of the blue, "You know, the Bible says that losing your virginity before you're married is a mortal sin." Deborah froze, excused herself, and went up to her room. She stayed up all night panicked by the conviction that her mother could somehow read her mind and knew that she had just had sex.

It is unlikely that Deborah's mother could read her mind, but Deborah's fear revealed how much she heard her mother's voice in her own mind, a voice that feared, prohibited, and hated sex. It was a voice that Deborah was to struggle with her entire life. It labeled her normal sexual desires as illicit and disgusting. It became part of a pathogenic belief that sexual pleasure leads to disaster. And underneath the harsh tone in her mother's voice lay a bitter unhappiness and envy born of lifelong sexual frustration. Deborah responded to this deeper level of meaning by feeling extremely guilty about enjoying a sexual life better than her mother's. On a symbolic level, uninhibited sexual pleasure felt like dancing on her mother's grave.

Deborah felt safe enough in a relationship to feel sexual, although this safety resulted from her compliance with her boyfriend's sexual needs. So attuned and responsive was she to the nuances of his erotic ups and downs that it was never clear to her whether she was having sex because she wanted to or because he did. Out in the public world, however, Deborah was so afraid of flaunting her considerable sex appeal that she completely avoided friendships with men and felt intensely uncomfortable when they flirted with her. As Deborah's therapy helped her feel less guilty about being attractive and assertive, a crisis suddenly occurred that crystallized her sexual conflicts.

Deborah became involved in a secure relationship with a man with whom she was falling in love. Their sexual relationship brought pleasure and satisfaction to both of them, although Deborah generally approached it with her characteristic geisha-like eagerness to please. One day Deborah met a man, a complete stranger, at a lunch counter and he began flirting with her. To her surprise, she discovered that she enjoyed the attention and she responded in kind. During this harmless banter Deborah suddenly had a panic attack, started hyperventilating, and felt claustrophobic and nauseated. She had to run from the restaurant and telephoned me reporting that she felt that she was going to die.

We talked at length about what had happened, and several issues became apparent. First, Deborah felt terribly guilty not only for talking to this man but for enjoying it, too. She said that something about it made her feel like a whore, despite the fact that she wasn't attracted to him at all. In fact, it was unclear to Deborah whether their flirtation was entirely authentic on her part, that is, whether her part in it was generated by her own autonomous interest in such play or by a compliance with what she sensed the man needed. Deborah became panicked because, on a symbolic level, she had entered a territory where her mother said she didn't belong and certainly where her mother didn't belong—namely, that of enjoying male attention outside her primary relationship. She wasn't supposed to enjoy being sexual in the world completely on her own, and when for a moment she seemed to do just that, she expected that something terrible would happen.

Both Jim and Deborah were guilty. Both worried about hurting their partners. Both had weak or unavailable parents. But the quality of experience underlying their sexual inhibitions was different. Unlike Deborah, Jim didn't fear sexual excitement itself, but his view of women as weak and cold created the conditions under which he could get aroused—namely, his breast fetish. Deborah was afraid of the power of her sexual feelings, worrying that unless they were controlled, they would destroy the relationships she valued most. She had to become an object of desire because the position of being a subject of desire was too frightening. Jim could become aroused through a fantasy of a woman wanting nothing more than his pleasure. For Deborah, sexual pleasure could be purchased only through a denial of her own needs.

CHAPTER 3

The Appeal of Pornography and Internet Sex

T MIGHT COME AS A SURPRISE to many people that something as "natural" as sexual arousal is so carefully constructed, with meanings that are central to our personalities. Many of these meanings involve beliefs about what it means to be a man or woman. It is my observation that everyone grows up forming a basic representation of men and women, mental pictures of what makes each gender tick, which guide us in our everyday interactions. Often, these pictures are unconscious and might even contradict one's rational view. For example, I have met several men who seem unconsciously to experience women as fundamentally weak or unhappy, and yet these are men who might well have conscious feelings of respect and admiration for their romantic partners or women they work with.

It is remarkable that behind something as simple as the image of a breast or an online role can lie a complicated story of trauma and transcendence. The psychoanalyst Robert Stoller called sexual markers such as large breasts "microdots," to convey the ways in which a mere detail is, in fact, a code for a complex and tension-filled life history. In that nanosecond between a man's perception of a shapely bosom and his feeling of psychological and sexual excitement lies the story of his entire psychological life.

One of the assumptions of my professional work is that each patient, each man in this case, has a very particular history and story that must be discovered to make sense of who he really is. However, there is great value in a theory that understands male sexual behavior in a way that, while allowing for enormous individual variation, sees what is common in the sexual psychology of all men, whether they are philanderers, construction workers whistling at women, men's movement devotees, Buddhist monks, Bill Clinton, Snoopy, or Dagwood Bumstead.

For example, as I've suggested, feelings of guilt and emotional isolation are common in men. In fact, guilt and loneliness almost always go together. A family in which guilt and an exaggerated sense of responsibility are likely to arise, a family in which one or both parents are unhappy and dependent on the children for their emotional well-being, is likely to produce children who feel lonely as well as guilty. After all, parents for whom children feel responsible are likely to be parents too emotionally impaired to attend properly to those children's needs. If the connection to someone's parents is based on fulfilling their needs, that child is likely to feel invisible because there is no room in the relationship for his or her real needs.

A colleague once suggested that, metaphorically, this is like imagining your parent sitting alone in the dark, shining a flashlight that cuts the darkness with a narrow beam of light. If you place yourself directly in this beam, the parent can see and connect with you; if not, you're in darkness and there is no relationship at all. If the son of such a parent was simply being himself, in other words, not addressing a pressing parental need, he would likely be in darkness. This darkness represents the internal sense of disconnectedness and emptiness that often coexists with problems of guilt and hyper-responsibility.

I can't emphasize enough how central this feeling of disconnectedness is in the minds and hearts of the men I treat. This core state of being is often difficult to see because some men, like my patient Joe, may appear to be robust and carefree on the outside while their inner feeling of alienation remains unrecognized. Often the men even hide these feelings from themselves because they believe sadness, depression, and emptiness are shameful.

For example, my patient, Joe—the "happily married man" with a penchant for prostitutes and Internet sex described in chapter 1—was raised by a father who reacted to signs of emotional need with impatience. While actually riddled with insecurity and fragility, Joe's father modeled a hyper-masculine ideal against which Joe frequently judged himself, and found himself to be lacking. Joe's interior emotional landscape was grim, but it took a long time before he could acknowledge that.

Joe eventually described his inner state this way:

I feel sometimes like the Lone Ranger, kind of heroic and strong when I'm working but then when I come home, I wonder about the purpose of things. My wife loves me, but sometimes she's like work; she requires interaction when all I want to do is be still in an environment that is taking care of me or at least not expecting anything of me. Then I feel peaceful but also lonely, so I'm sort of damned if I do, damned if I don't. Sometimes I feel like when I'm around people, I'm putting on a show, but then I wonder, well, do I want to be alone my whole life? In those moments, I feel kind of grim and like the world is a bit grim and sad.

Although Joe turned out to be an unusually self-reflective and articulate patient and certainly had his own idiosyncrasies, his depiction of his inner life would feel familiar to many of my male patients.

Depression, feelings of low self-esteem or rejection, and loneliness are incompatible with sexual arousal. Prostitutes and cybersex were Joe's solution. In a way, he "treated" his underlying depression with sexual fantasies and arousal. Since the problem involved feeling cut off from people, the interactive nature of the fantasies that Joe enacted, on- and off-line, were crucial to his sexual satisfactions. The boy sitting alone in his bedroom feeling that he was completely off his parents' emotional radar screens could not have felt deserving of pleasure, confident about his desirability, or sexually potent. Joe's innermost view of relationships was that they were one-way streets going the wrong way, and that the caretaking he sometimes got from others was transient and ultimately not attuned to him.

Another patient, Gerard, was exquisitely sensitive to the ebb and flow of his wife's sexual ardor. When asked about how things were going at home, Gerard would always answer in terms of how frequently he and his wife were having sex. For him, sexual activity was the primary barometer by which he measured the state of his marriage. Gerard had been raised by a single mother who was competent and efficient but utterly unable to be nurturing. By the time he reached adolescence, Gerard had discovered sex and reported the astounding fact that in his last two years of high school he was having sex five or six times per week. He was "treating" painful feelings of emptiness at home with the pleasures and connection he found in sexual activity.

Loneliness and rejection often drive and shape sexual desire, especially in men. Many of the most common male sexual fantasies, practices, and preferences can be understood as attempts to counteract these feelings and their accompanying beliefs. Internet pornography and sex is one such attempt. Joe often went online to masturbate late in the evening when his wife had gone to sleep, or on weekends when he was home alone. He would go to several chat rooms where he had developed sexual relationships with women, always using pseudonyms. It is often said that one of the wrinkles of cybersex is that no one ever knows who his partner really is, or even if that person is male or female. Joe came to feel that he could always tell the sex of the other person and that, even if there was some small doubt, it didn't really matter to him. He knew he was enacting a fantasy and was happy surrendering to it.

These interactions in the chat rooms, while varied, tended to have the same structure. Joe was the aggressor, the initiator. He would start to narrate to the woman what he wanted to do—for example, that he wanted to "suck her tits" or "press his cock against her ass." If his prospective cyber-partner was interested, she would immediately respond by telling Joe how much that excited her. He would then go on to describe how he would have sex with her, step by step. Often these scenarios were quasi-rapes, but the crucial requirement to Joe was that the woman frequently indicated how aroused she was by what he was doing and by his penis. If she tried to take too much control of the interaction or didn't respond with enough expressions of pleasure, his excitement would diminish and he would seek satisfaction elsewhere.

Joe enjoyed these encounters and didn't want them to end; they weren't "quickies" designed to help him masturbate as fast as possible. He liked to maintain the tension and the excitement. Sometimes he had a full erection and other times he didn't. Sometimes he would touch himself and other times not. His physical arousal was, for the most part, maintained at a low to moderate level, with various "spikes" that corresponded to moments when the imaginary action was especially vivid. Eventually, Joe would physically masturbate to orgasm. Immediately afterward, he would completely lose interest and turn off his computer.

It was crucial to Joe that the cybersex experience was interactive because only then could he really feel that he was related and not alone. There had to be an actual person on the other end of his DSL line rather than simply a two-dimensional picture. The anonymity of the interaction, however, was also necessary because it freed Joe from the potential danger of feeling responsible for the other person's feelings and satisfaction. He could always find someone who sufficiently shared his particular fantasies so that he would never have to feel he had to sacrifice his own needs or pleasures for those of another, a danger that was too often present in normal sexual interactions. It was important that his cyberpartners validate his uniqueness by reassuring Joe that they were aroused by him, that the connection was intense, and that they were satisfied. There was no negotiation—if the cyberpartner didn't want to play in exactly his way, he'd simply hit the delete key.

The relief that Joe found in cybersex was due to the potent way it addressed his loneliness. Experts on sexual addictions often argue that the types of sexual relationships that Joe found on the Internet are not real relationships and that, therefore, Joe's "relief" was illusory. I would say that it was temporary but not at all illusory. When Joe was instant messaging with someone playing the role of a sexually submissive young woman, for example, he depended on the fact that there was another person there; the conversations had the same structure and content as any other, more "real" conversation might have, and the possibilities of understanding and misunderstanding, of more or less empathic connection, were similar as well.

And yet, such interactive cyber-relationships play with but don't conform to reality. They are simultaneously real and not real, intensely personal and completely anonymous, connected to others and private. They are somewhere in the middle of a sexual continuum that ranges from solitary masturbatory fantasy to true mature relatedness in which each person fully appreciates the other's difference. Sexual opportunities on the Internet are complex and varied, although all of them fall on this spectrum from the static and two-dimensional to the psychologically three-dimensional and interpersonal. Here is a list of Web-based sexual possibilities:

1. Traditional pornographic pictures of men and women of every kind, age, shape, and in every sexual position imaginable.
2. Streaming video of porn stars.
3. Streaming video made by amateurs of "average" people, heightening the viewer's experience of it as "real."
4. Interactive DVDs, played on a computer, with special software programs that enable the viewers to feel as if they are actually sexually interacting with the professional models on the screen.
5. Live audio and video streams of women acting in sexually suggestive ways in real time, including the so-called sex-cams broadcasting from a woman's bedroom. Some of these performances allow for viewer and performer to simultaneously interact via their keyboards.

The viewer, for a price, may suggest certain behaviors to the woman, making the experience more interactive. These performances may be offered to a group or to an individual.

6. On the level of the written word, there is, of course, e-mail, which is relational and can be highly erotic, although the waiting time between posting and response may be long.

7. Bulletin boards on which someone can post his or her erotic interest or fantasy and get responses from others with similar interests, generating a sequential online conversation.

8. Instant messaging technologies with which people can have live erotic conversations in real time.

9. Direct video-based one-on-one sexual interactions (not yet widely available).

10. Teledildonics—a technology in which each person wears a body suit with strategically placed sensors and stimulators that can be activated by one's partner via the computer connection (not yet widely available).

Along this spectrum, more and more "reality," more and more actual relatedness, is available.

In Joe's online affairs, he needed his partners to have their own sexual agency—they couldn't simply mirror his own desire—but he also had to control the interactions. Since the feeling of connectedness was crucial, he preferred the interactive modalities. These included instant messaging and bulletin boards, as well as private shows with porn stars in real time in which conversations between viewer and performer are made possible via keyboard. Consumers of sex on the Internet have a wide choice of modalities and products. To an important degree, the choice of modality is influenced by how much of a "real" connection a user wants and needs. The kind of interactive connection that Joe needed would be much too anxiety-provoking for someone else with other needs, for example, someone for whom any independence in the cyberpartner would lead to fears of being controlled, judged, or rejected.

Whether on- or off-line, every sexual activity or fantasy falls somewhere on this continuum of control and independence. When Joe was with a prostitute, the independent external agency of the woman was powerful, and if she was able to divine and serve his interests, the result was an especially satisfying sexual connection. On the other hand, some prostitutes had reactions that were too independent for Joe. For example, sometimes they didn't act especially excited, were too financially greedy, or couldn't play the roles that Joe required. Joe's pleasure decreased accordingly. On the other end of the spectrum was Joe's collection of pornographic pictures. Here there was no danger at all of the women having any independent subjectivity, and so they were completely safe in that regard. But he found these experiences somewhat boring because they lacked the intensity of a real connection.

Joe liked the feeling of connection, even if he knew all the while that the object of his desire was not really who she was pretending to be. It didn't matter to him that the prostitute was just doing her job or that the woman with the screen name *Vixen69* might really be a seventeen-year-old boy from Poland. Joe suspended reality for the purpose of sexual pleasure. While it may seem peculiar that Joe could ignore such basic realities as the age and sex of his online sexual partner, this denial is really just an exaggeration of a normal ingredient of sexual fantasies of all kinds. After all, what is the status of reality when a man becomes aroused by a woman passing by in stiletto heels? She is suggesting a fantasy to him, a fantasy in which she is tough and sexy. In this sense, stiletto heels are like a screen name—a marker for a particular sexual fantasy. The particular woman wearing the heels may "in reality" be the opposite of tough and sexy, and the man may even know this, and yet this reality doesn't matter because at the moment of arousal he is engaged in an imaginary relationship that has just the right ingredients he needs to get aroused. It's as if his mind is operating on parallel planes. On one level, he lets himself completely believe that she is, say, a dominatrix, and on another he may know her really to be shy and inhibited.

Thus, the difference between a real woman with high heels passing by and someone playing a woman with high heels in a chat room may be less than meets the eye. The former is real in the sense of existing in corporeal form right before the man's eyes, although the psychic drama in which she plays a role, the fantasy she elicits, is entirely in his mind. The woman in the chat room seems to be a figment of the imagination in that one doesn't have any idea what she really looks like and, in this sense, doesn't exist as a real being in physical space. And yet, she may bring much more of a spontaneous and real personality to the experience than the passerby in high heels. The passerby might as well be a two-dimensional billboard, while the cyberpartner is quite human. Which is more real?

The British psychoanalyst D. W. Winnicott called the types of experiences in which reality is both acknowledged and voluntarily suspended "transitional spaces." He posited that a baby's stuffed animal or blanket could at once symbolize something external and something that is a part of the child. Winnicott meant that the child experiences these early playthings simultaneously as extensions of him- or herself and things that are "out there" in the world. At this age and stage of development, Winnicott argued, this ambiguity between inside and outside, between something being under one's control and being independent, is healthy and normal. The caretaker does not question or attempt to resolve this ambiguity for the child. The blanket replaces the mother's comfort, and yet is still "only" a blanket, and child and mother need not clarify it further. Most forms of play fit into this category. Children pretend that they are space aliens and fighter pilots, become fiercely involved in the reality of the roles, and yet simultaneously know that it's only a game.

Sexual fantasies, when enacted, can also fall into this category. When Joe asked a prostitute to play the role of a seductive cheerleader, he and she were creating a transitional space in which he could both invest a relationship with reality and simultaneously know that it was a pretense. Joe felt no contradiction here at all. Instead, he was able to suspend his reality testing and allow himself to believe in the situation enough to get aroused in a very real sense. The physical reality of his sexual excitement reflected the fact that he and she had created a space safe enough for him to play out his cheerleader fantasy. As with other male consumers of the sex industry, Joe knew that the woman was simply acting, but it didn't matter. Her actions matched his desires, and he never felt the need to question her authenticity.

Some men cannot tolerate the tension between reality and fantasy enough to experience sexual pleasure in these ways. For these men, it matters that the woman online or in the massage parlor is not really aroused. They need to make the interaction more realistic. For example, they might ask the woman servicing them out on a real date, or pressure their online chat partners to meet them in person. Such men can accept only a reality that is concrete or literal and cannot play with it. Other men, of course, have the opposite sensitivity. They cannot tolerate very much reality in their sexual fantasy life and therefore don't ever actualize or enact it in the ways that Joe did. They certainly couldn't see a prostitute, because she would inevitability make it too real—even the reality of her corporeal being ruins the daydream for these men. Such men can tolerate online women better than fully embodied ones, although they gravitate toward photographs and movies more than interactive modalities for fear of having to encounter a woman who is real in her own right.

My patient Paul was a good example of men who can't tolerate the ambiguity of transitional space. Paul's special sexual interest involved not cybersex but frequenting brothels instead. He told me that he always chose black women to have sex with because, he confessed, he thought that they were more likely to "want to have a good time." When he first told me about these encounters, he always implied that, while he realized that they were just doing their job, he believed that they really enjoyed it with him.

The psychological meaning of these encounters was complex. First, Paul associated blackness with uninhibited sexuality, an association that also reflects the belief in the dominant white culture that people of color are highly sexed. In addition, the devalued social status of the prostitute and her race functioned as an antidote to his tendency to worry about women and to feel judged by them. After all, his unconscious mind reasoned, since she is already devalued, he didn't have to worry about demeaning her, and in addition, he didn't have to worry about the judgments and feelings of someone beneath him. But Paul needed the feeling of connection as well, and he needed to believe that she was genuinely excited by him, that what he saw was real. Paul couldn't pretend. The pathogenic beliefs against which he was struggling, the beliefs that women were too self-preoccupied to care about him and instead were brittle and difficult to please, were so strong that he had to deny the pretend aspect of the connection and insist that it was real to both himself and his partners.

Paul's inability to tolerate the imaginary dimension of a sexual interaction is frequently seen in the reports that other men give of the sexual pleasure enjoyed by a prostitute or other sex worker that they have hired. Like Paul, such men need to believe that the woman they have hired is becoming aroused and having bona fide orgasms. For example, on a website devoted to "consumer reviews" of sexual escorts, the following depictions are given of the authenticity of one escort's sexual responses: "She is definitely into it." "It seemed she was enjoying everything as much as I." "I worked her clit for a quick 'O' and then gave her another one a few minutes later." "She apologized unnecessarily for getting lost in her own pleasure."

Sometimes, the male reviewer will qualify his assertion that the escort had an orgasm by including, parenthetically, something like "unless she was the best actress who ever lived." Such caveats are added, of course, to protect the man against appearing to be foolishly taken in, but there is no doubt that the man believes that the orgasms were genuine.

Of course, there may well be times when a sex worker derives sexual pleasure, perhaps even an orgasm, from a client, but according to most accounts, the occurrence is rare. What is not rare, however, is the need of this type of man to ward off the dangers of feeling invisible and disconnected by believing in the reality of her pleasure. Ambiguity cannot be tolerated; transitional space cannot be maintained. The "truth" of the matter must be asserted and defended.

At the other end of the spectrum we find men who can't tolerate too much reality at all. Kent was one such man. He was afraid of sexualized interactions of almost any kind in almost any situation. His fantasy life, however, was rich and preoccupied him much of the time. Kent couldn't or wouldn't describe his sexual fantasies in any detail—or perhaps there weren't any details to tell. What he thought about, he said, were images of having sex with several happy women at the same time. The feeling in the daydream was always light and playful, and he was completely at ease. That's all Kent could say on the subject. In contrast to Paul, who tried always to impose his inner life on the external world, Kent retreated completely from the external world and contented himself with an internal world in which he felt entirely safe. He couldn't easily sexualize real women because of his pathogenic belief that women basically hated men and would humiliate them if given half a chance. His mother had done just this throughout his childhood, both to his father and him, and his default picture of women was that they were highly malevolent. His fantasy life was the opposite, populated as it was by happy women who wanted nothing more than a playful sexual mutuality.

Both Paul and Kent had sexual fantasies that were arousing because they disproved their underlying pathogenic belief that they were fundamentally alone in a cold world. Paul needed a realistic interaction with a female figure to counteract his disconnectedness, while Kent did it via an entirely private daydream. Their differences had to do with idiosyncratic personality factors, not with the basic dynamics of their sexual arousal.

Sexual Addiction

Regardless of whether one prefers Internet sex that is pictorial or interactive, this new medium is powerfully compelling as a source of gratification because it is entirely private and anonymous and therefore enables users to circumvent the inhibiting effects of their own conscience and the opinions of others. For some people, it is so compelling that it comes to dominate their lives.

I have treated several men who might be described as cybersex addicts. In today's world of twelve-step programs designed to address almost every compulsion, sex addiction is frequently mentioned as a growing problem, particularly pornography and cybersex addiction. Some researchers define Internet addiction as spending more than ten hours per week online involved in activities of a sexual nature, when such activities feel compulsive and interfere in some way with a person's work or personal life. On the basis of this definition, it may well be that there are millions of people, mostly men, who suffer from this malady. Obviously there is no hard and fast limit beyond which Internet sex is pathological, but such attempts at definition serve the purpose of pointing out that the availability of sex over the Internet has created problems for some men.

My patient David was one such man. He was single and lived alone but actively dated. He came to see me for help regarding his compulsive sexual use of the Internet. By his report (probably an underestimation), David spent about thirty hours per week seeking or having sexual experiences online. He joked that given the strain that such activity put on his hands, both by typing and masturbating, it was a wonder he didn't develop a repetitive stress injury! While David frequently visited Internet sites that featured sexually explicit pictures and videos, he was especially drawn to chat rooms and bulletin boards where he could sexually interact with real women, or at least with people who used the screen names of real women. Like Joe, David didn't care if his correspondents were actually male or female, as long as they convincingly enacted the role of a woman doing the types of things he wanted. He had some regulars he met in particular rooms or on special boards, and if they were unavailable, he would cruise these rooms and proposition women with the beginning of a fantasy to see if they were interested.

David's fantasies were all mildly sadomasochistic. For example, he might approach a woman online and say something like: "I'm having a fantasy about you. . . . I want you to spread your legs while remaining sitting right where you are. . . . Interested?" If the woman's own preferred sexual fantasy was piqued by this invitation, she might respond with something like: "Yes . . . I'm at work at the moment. . . . Do you want me to do it right here in the office?" And this is how the interaction would begin. He would usually direct the fantasy, for example, telling her to hike up her dress slowly, or to start masturbating under her desk as colleagues worked. Or, he would approach a potential online liaison with some other fantasy, fishing for a connection. If he didn't like the results, he would simply block any further correspondence and go on to the next.

David would surf the Internet and have online conversations like this for hours. He would enter what he called "the zone." This zone was an almost trancelike state in which he was aroused, but not to orgasm. Often he was only the slightest bit tumescent, with occasional spikes in arousal and then deflations. He described the experience as frustrating but totally absorbing. Part of the reason that interactive cybersex didn't bring him steadily to climax is that he'd have to wait for written responses and often could not count on the responses being good enough to fit into his preferred scenarios. He had the feeling that he was always probing, working, looking for more intense stimulation. He likened the experience to chasing a cocaine high. He'd go from partner to partner, sometimes using the wonders of computer windows to carry on two or three conversations at once. After a while, sometimes a long while, David would decide to masturbate to completion with one of his cyberpartners, although this, too, proceeded in fits and starts, in part, he said, because of "the problem of typing with one hand." He'd type something, then stroke himself, watch for the reply, and then have to stop and type some more to keep it going. Eventually, David would have an orgasm and immediately log off.

After each one of these sessions, David felt slightly down. He couldn't believe that he had been online for so long, often feeling the kind of guilt and chagrin heard from an alcoholic after a bender. The "down" was not just his guilt speaking; it also reflected the underlying emotional state that the cybersex seemed unconsciously intended to alleviate. I would describe that state as one of depressive disconnection, something that David, like Joe and many of the other men I've treated, had struggled with his entire life. Over and over on his computer screen, David would attempt to play out his ruthlessness and find someone who loved it rather than rejected it, who became aroused and not hurt by his aggressive desires. When he found such a woman, he felt stimulated, and this state was powerfully attractive to him. In this state, David wasn't alone, he was connected to a woman who was excited to connect with him, who fully welcomed the desires and wishes about which he felt the most guilt and shame and who wasn't hurt by them. He wanted the connection to continue, didn't really want to have an orgasm until, finally, the frustration and sheer fatigue of it all made it necessary.

David required the anonymity of the Internet and the fictitious quality of the transient relationships he found there in order to feel safe enough to express his innermost fantasies. He also required the live-ness, the real-ness, of having a conversation with an actual person to counteract his detached and depressive baseline mood. He needed it to be real and yet not real. A prostitute would have been too real; a pornographic picture was too unreal. Interactive cybersex was a perfect compromise, ambiguous enough to allow him to enjoy a connection in a safe way.

The delay built in to even the most directly interactive Internet communication highlights one of its "not-real" dimensions and is worth exploring further. A completely real sexual relationship, after all, is mediated by speaking and touching, while the Internet is limited to some degree by the ability of each partner to type. David, for example, complained that some of his cyberpartners seemed to complement his sexual fantasies perfectly but that their slow typing made their Internet sex frustrating.

David described one interaction that neatly illustrates the ingredients necessary to sustain the ambiguity of interactive cybersex. He was enjoying an erotic conversation online with someone with the screen name *Tania69*, a conversation in which they were enacting roles of extreme dominance and submission. David was "forcing" Tania into more and more degrading situations in which he was sexually controlling and abusing her, all of which was tremendously exciting to him—and apparently to Tania69. At one point, Tania said that she was so hot that she wanted to speak directly to him. David reluctantly agreed, instantly apprehensive that the introduction of this new level of reality would create a type of performance anxiety in him that interactions via keyboards kept at bay.

As they began to speak on the phone, David's fears materialized. Tania's voice was more gruff than he had imagined, and she seemed anything but submissive. As he began to order her around, much as he had been doing online, something in the way he did so was apparently unconvincing to Tania, who began to indicate that he was being "too nice." In response to the feeling that he was now letting her down, David's arousal diminished, which made him less passionate in his role, and the interaction soon fizzled out. The imaginative role relationship that they had both created on the Internet and that more than adequately enabled David to overcome his tendency to worry about pleasing women could not be sustained under the weight of the greater reality of spoken contact.

It would be as if, while playing with a child using toy spaceships, one were to say, "You know, these are just toys. They can't really fly, can they?" Such an insistence on greater material reality would undermine the suspension of disbelief necessary for the game to be fun. Similarly, the written dimension of cybersex, while not real enough because of the limitations of the written word, also enables a greater suspension of disbelief than do more direct forms of communication.

Such a confluence of reality and fantasy, experienced in the anonymity of the Internet, is a powerful tonic for people who feel psychologically disconnected and who are consciously or unconsciously guilty about their desires, worried about hurting others or being rejected by them. No wonder sex on the Internet is so popular and becoming more so. It offers a sexual relief from the loneliness and guilt that so many men experience. It provides a safe haven within which men can feel connected and have their needs met by women who want nothing more than to make them happy. It can be accessed in complete privacy and enjoyed in the time and place and manner of the user's own choosing.

Another one of the Internet's special features is its tendency to promote an escalation of sexual experimentation. Many of my male patients who are regular Internet users report that their fantasies often undergo an evolution. Because they can gratify any fantasy without fear of exposure, there is an inherent tendency for the threshold of pleasure to go up. Once one sexual taboo is overcome, the user is tempted to challenge others. It is as if the Internet offers these men an ever-expanding range of sexual possibilities—images, scenarios, role-plays, and other forms of sexual experience—that capture their core fantasies in increasingly extreme and precise ways. This is precisely why Internet sex can quickly become so appealing to some men.

For example, my patient Benny was sexually preoccupied with breasts. When he first discovered sex on the Internet, he merely downloaded pictures of women with large breasts and used these images to masturbate. As time went on, however, the anonymity of the Internet provided a safe cover for him to seek out more extreme variations of his particular fetish. He discovered websites devoted to lactating women, others focusing on "tit torture," in which women's breasts were bound or squeezed, and eventually began to visit websites specializing in explicit incest scenarios. The original object of his sexual fascination—simple pictures of large-breasted women—came to feel boring, and he began experimenting with increasingly taboo and forbidden scenarios to get aroused.

The question of whether this process of sexual escalation poses a danger to the men engaging in it, to their partners, or to society is a complicated one. My clinical experience tells me that most of these men are rooted enough in reality, and derive enough satisfaction and pleasure from their real relationships, that they are in little danger of becoming involved in Internet sex in ways that are destructive to themselves or others (e.g., pushing cybersexual relationships into real social ones or spending so much time online that work and family lives begin to practically suffer). The opportunity that cybersex offers to break taboos is usually not compelling enough to draw men away from their real-world gratifications and interests. Real relationships still trump virtual ones.

For some men, however, the availability of taboo forms of sexual pleasure on their computer monitors is a siren's call, and such men can become obsessed with cybersex to a degree that feels painful and has negative consequences psychologically and socially. What seems to differentiate these men from others who might only be interested in Internet sex but not consumed by it, is that the former have a deeper and more traumatic sense of disconnectedness and an emotional life that is more impoverished than that of ordinary men. Regardless of what it looks like to the outside observer, the men who risk their marriages or jobs because of their overinvolvement in cybersex have found a solution to their internal problems of loneliness and guilt that is so pleasurably intense as to render any real-world excitement pale in comparison.

It could certainly be argued that cybersex is not to blame here because these men are not really making a choice between cybersex and healthier relatedness, and that in the absence of the Internet they would turn to traditional forms of pornography or else go through their lives basically haunted by a grim internal world. However, this argument is weak. Addictive sexual use of the Internet often actively drives away potential sources of comfort and support (for example, family members and friends), and therefore actively encourages greater social isolation. In other words, when these men choose the Internet they make more realistic solutions less likely. Further, in the absence of the dangerous social consequences of extreme Internet use, such men are not motivated to get the professional help they might need. Suffering is not the key to therapeutic change, but it certainly helps in getting someone to a therapist's door in the first place. The intense appeal of cybersex, then, might make getting help even less probable.

I've helped several men who only came to see me because they were forced to do so by their wives. In each case, their partners discovered either an online affair or evidence of sexual obsessions of some kind on their computers. These men would never have sought out psychotherapeutic help on their own because their addictive use of sexual outlets available on the Internet were pleasurable and vital enough to make "treatment" feel like a threat to their basic way of life.

Why can't these men who are flocking to the Internet to seek connection and stimulation accomplish the same thing with real women? And what can we say about the mental health of someone like David who clearly feels himself in the grip of a compulsion that tyrannizes him as much as it gratifies him? The problem with men like David is that their pathogenic beliefs about what they can expect from women are deep and highly resistant to being negated by experience with real women. As with other solutions to disconnectedness like drugs or alcohol, the relief that cybersex provides is immediate, powerful, and completely under the man's control. Unlike real women, virtual women can't be hurt, they're always there, they never reject you, and they want nothing more than to make you happy.

How Much Should Women Worry about Internet Sex?

There are no simple answers to questions about the potential harm of cybersex. The man who becomes obsessed with Internet sex or even has an actual affair because of his longing for a connection free of responsibility and worry may not be motivated at all by a wish to hurt himself or his wife, but his actions can clearly do both. It can psychologically hurt him in the sense that it can reinforce an irrational but unconscious belief that he is fated to be unable to enjoy sex with someone he also loves and is dependent on. I would view this as a pathogenic belief that could be altered in psychotherapy, which would free this man to have a fuller and happier marriage. But men who act out in these compulsive ways rarely seek psychotherapy because they don't believe that there is any other way of looking at the world. Further, I have certainly seen countless men who come into therapy convinced that their wives wouldn't do, much less enjoy, something that they see portrayed in their pornography, only to find that when they talk to their wives about their fantasies the response is unexpectedly positive. One might say that the involvement of these men in pornography and infidelity sold themselves and their partners short. In this sense, a man's fantasies might also be deemed harmful.

I remember a patient, Michael, who claimed that the reason he collected pornography and visited prostitutes was because his wife was sexually "uptight." He attributed her inhibitions to the fact that she was an ardent feminist who reacted angrily when she felt objectified in any way. In fact, when I saw both of them together, an entirely different story emerged. It turned out that Michael's wife acted "uptight" because she felt chronically rejected by Michael, especially in the bedroom. When Michael began to act more loving and then revealed some of his kinkier fantasies to her, his wife was surprisingly receptive. Michael was clearly a victim of his own self-fulfilling expectations.

While cybersex may or may not be intrinsically harmful to its male consumers and their real-world partners, understanding its dynamics is almost always useful. I treated a man, Jeff, whose wife had recently discovered that he had been regularly having sexual conversations with women on the Internet. Jeff's wife was hurt and horrified, and he was stricken with guilt and panic over her threats of divorce. Jeff dated the beginning of his intense Internet use to the period following the birth of his second child, a period also marked by a serious health scare for him. He described a growing sense of estrangement from his wife, an increased sense of loneliness, and a growing feeling of financial and familial responsibility. His wife, Jeff said, was unsympathetic about his medical concerns, and increasingly critical of his performance as a father and a provider. Jeff told me that he felt like a camel in his life, going for long distances without any nourishment, anxiously working hard to "do the right thing" without much encouragement at home. He reported that his wife was sexually passive and both unwilling and uninterested in any sexual experimentation.

Without knowing for sure whether these depictions of his wife were actually true, it became clear to me that they were certainly familiar to Jeff. His descriptions of his wife bore a strong resemblance to those of his mother. Jeff described his mother as a critical and narcissistic woman, impossible to satisfy and readily feeling abandoned by any signs of her son's independence. Jeff felt like he was on a never-ending and unrewarding treadmill when it came to women.

In chat rooms, Jeff found the antidote to this treadmill. In his sexual and masturbatory conversations with women there, he felt connected, appreciated, and free. The women with whom he corresponded were always both eager to please and easily pleased themselves. He felt he could assert himself and his needs without guilt. He could talk dirty. He could experiment with scenarios that were sadomasochistic in nature. He could be ruthless and his partners would love it rather than feel rejected or burdened. His virtual relationships counteracted his pathogenic beliefs that women were hard to please, easily hurt, and inherently sexually inhibited.

Fortunately for Jeff, his wife didn't leave him over her discoveries. She was hurt and furious, to be sure, but she was also willing to try to understand the meaning of his actions. She went into therapy herself and dragged

Jeff in with her. What was most striking, however, was the surprising fact that their sex life opened up in frequency, intensity, and variety. They became closer than ever before. What accounted for this unexpected change?

First, upon learning more about his default beliefs about women, Jeff was able to both talk about and test them with his wife. His wife revealed that she, too, had been feeling lonely and desperately wanted Jeff to be more assertive in the bedroom. She wanted to experiment more, but had worried that Jeff would be offended! Further, she acknowledged that she was overly critical at times and understood that this could lead Jeff to shut down, but she went on to encourage him to stand up to her, that contrary to his expectations, she would be relieved and not hurt by his self-assertion. Jeff was surprised and delighted by these conversations and began to initiate sex more. True to her word, his wife responded. Jeff felt as though he had died and gone to sexual heaven.

The second reason that Jeff's marital crisis led to a sexual renaissance was that his wife paradoxically, but unconsciously, felt freed up by her husband's betrayal. Because Jeff was so clearly in the wrong, his wife could give up inhibitions based on her own guilty belief that Jeff would reject her or be repelled by her sexuality. In other words, she had nothing to lose. She now had the moral high ground. She could afford to "let the cat out of the bag" because she was free of any fear of moral judgment or abandonment. Jeff was on the ropes, and his wife could be sexually ruthless with impunity.

This situation was, of course, far more complicated than I've described. The point of this story is that when men are not encouraged or even forced to examine the psychological dynamics underlying their cybersex use, they can easily live their lives entirely in the grips of harmful pathogenic beliefs about what real women want, beliefs that prevent them from having fuller romantic and sexual lives.

Feeling that they're unable to compete with fantasies available on the Internet, many women have viewed the growing popularity of cybersex with alarm, fearing that cybersex will encourage a new wave of male infidelity and abandonment. Certainly, men like David can become obsessed with the opportunities available online to gratify a range of fantasies that they feel too guilty to indulge in their relationships with real women. If a man is not motivated to explore the meanings of his sexuality, or to use his Internet preferences as windows through which he can better understand his psychology, then online sexual indulgences may well become so attractive that they take up increasing amounts of energy that might otherwise be directed toward developing real relationships. In this sense, the availability of cybersex can become a problem in relationships and families.

However, a number of cautions must be added to this growing alarm about cybersex and cyber-addiction. First, as Alvin Cooper, PhD, former director of the San Jose Marital and Sexuality Center in Santa Clara, California, has demonstrated in his research on men who use the Internet for sexual stimulation, only a small percentage of men seem to be susceptible to using it in addictive ways. Second, one has to ask what the men who withdraw from their partners and families and reserve their sexual passion for the Internet would otherwise be doing if the Internet didn't exist. Would they be having affairs? Would they be any less sexually inhibited or emotionally unavailable? Would they redirect the energy now used for online satisfactions back into their primary relationships? Would the absence of opportunities to sexually surmount their loneliness and guilt online force them to finally confront what ails them, get into therapy, or insist that their real relationships improve?

My experience tells me that reducing a man's sexual outlets does not increase the probability that he will be or act any healthier. He will still feel disconnected, still retreat into fantasy, and still withdraw from relationships in which he feels burdened with guilt, worry, and rejection. In this sense, cybersex is more of a symptom than the cause of the difficulties that many men have in being sexually intimate with their wives. Cybersex, like pornography in general, offers an escape, an imaginary and temporary resolution to inhibitions about sexual ruthlessness and relatedness that are deeply rooted in the psychological makeup of many men in our society. In this sense, unless cybersex is sought out to such a degree that the actual time investment literally interferes with the maintenance of relationships or work, it does not necessarily represent a growing threat to women and to relationships.

This is not to say, of course, that a woman shouldn't feel threatened by the discovery that her husband or boyfriend is visiting Internet porn sites or having cybersex online with real women. It would be difficult to imagine any woman not having a problem with these activities, particularly if her partner is less than fully involved, sexually or otherwise, with her. After all, the man appears to be having sex with someone else, regardless of the psychological meaning of that encounter to him. How could a woman accept the excuse that such encounters are not taking anything away from her?

The issue is not that cybersex is good or bad, but that, in these cases, it has different meanings to the man engaging in it and the woman reacting to it. Both meanings are valid and have to be taken into account if this issue is to be resolved. For the man, the appeal of cybersex lies in its not being real; for women the threat lies in its reality. The difference reflects the essential ambiguity of the experience to begin with—part real, part imaginary. To the extent that Internet sex, particularly the interactive variety, conveys a sense of relatedness, it counteracts the man's disconnectedness and threatens his partner with rejection. And to the extent that it is anonymous and based on wishful fantasy, cybersex counteracts the man's guilt about his sexual ruthlessness and his fears of being invisible, and poses no threat at all to his partner. Both are true, and both need to be taken into account in any theory about the meaning of Internet sexuality.

Thus far, women do not seem to be in danger of becoming obsessed with Internet sex. However, for better or worse, women are getting involved in cybersex in increasing numbers, although given the anonymity afforded by the medium it is impossible to assess gender differences with any precision. In an online survey conducted in 2001–2002, Alvin Cooper estimated that women accounted for about 10 percent of those who confessed to spending excessive time involved in cybersex. My clinical experience suggests that this figure is now much higher. Since women are, on the whole, more drawn to relationships than men are, they seem to be drawn more to sexual opportunities on the Internet that are interactive, modalities such as Instant Messaging, bulletin boards, and chat rooms.

Women go online for sexual gratification for many of the same reasons as men, namely, to find a psychic (albeit momentary) cure for their loneliness and guilt and to use the Internet as a safe outlet for their sexual desires. Instead of being shut down by guilt over their ruthlessness or sexually inhibited because of fears of rejection, women can now participate in forbidden forms of sexuality. This is especially important to women who are hobbled by the chilling effects of survivor guilt and about being stronger and having more pleasure than their mothers.

The fact that more women are not flocking to online sexual sites and interactive outlets reflects their fear and dislike of having sex outside relationships. This attitude is both a strength and weakness for women. On the one hand, women's sexuality tends to be embedded in relationships and, as a result, can foster deeper forms of mutuality and erotic connection than can the sexuality of many men. On the other hand, women's fears about enjoying sex for its own sake may result from an inordinate amount of guilt about their capacity for sexual ruthlessness, and thus come at the cost of deeper pleasures. This latter possibility accounts for Cooper's observation that women tend to try to push their cybersex relationships out into the "real" world, as opposed to men who traditionally are more visual and so are enamored of pictures and video sites on the Internet.

The question of whether the growing sexual appeal of the Internet is good or bad for our culture is the most difficult to answer. It is a question that is being hotly debated by feminist theorists, pundits, and conservative critics, many of whom claim that cybersex is bad, immoral, and likely to reinforce harmful attitudes toward women and children, including objectification, rape, and pedophilia. I do not agree. There has not been a single controlled study that has demonstrated a long-term increase in the incidence or intensity of these attitudes in the real world as a result of exposure to sexual content on the Internet. It is true, for example, that pedophiles usually consume child pornography and are often heavily involved in both its collection and dissemination on the Internet, and a small number of such men probably use this new digital medium to find potential objects for their desire. It has also been demonstrated that rapists often have been deeply involved in the world of pornography before and during the periods of their criminal activity. But the fact that rapists and pedophiles like cybersex and pornography is irrelevant to the question of the harm of such sexual media, because correlation is not causation. For example, it might be shown that serial killers often have a history of drug abuse. It does not follow that drugs cause killing sprees, because it is likely that other factors like childhood abuse, the availability of guns, and socioeconomic class are at least as much correlated with this gruesome behavior, if not more. Similarly, it might be argued, frequent pornography use and sex crimes might be correlated, but both might be related to some third factor, for example, certain pathological family dynamics or social experiences.

I would argue that the increasing use of the Internet for sexual purposes is not, in and of itself, an intrinsically harmful social trend. The medium itself does not carry an intrinsic moral position, but interacts with the complex psyches and culture of its users.

Sexual Boredom
and Infidelity

WITH MEN STRUGGLING TO OVERCOME GUILT and loneliness and women increasingly feeling entitled to take charge of and fully enjoy their own sexuality, it is no wonder that many couples suffer from problems in the bedroom. In my professional experience, each sex tends to have characteristic complaints about the other's sexuality. Women complain that men either don't want to have sex enough or they want it too much, that they aren't intimate enough during and after sex, and that they are drawn to younger women and are therefore vulnerable to having affairs. Men complain about the frequency and intensity of their partners' desire, as well as the latter's unwillingness to sexually experiment. Given my focus on male sexuality, however, and because I believe that male sexuality is so often misunderstood, this chapter will emphasize the psychological roots of the male sexual attitudes and behavior that seem most often to create problems in relationships.

The most shameful secret of a relationship often involves the frequency—or lack thereof—of sex. A patient may readily reveal that his or her spouse is withdrawn, rejecting, unfaithful, or otherwise abusive but will be embarrassed to mention that they haven't had sex in three months. Notwithstanding the fact that the problem of sexual boredom seems to grace the covers of *Newsweek* and *Time* magazines every year, and despite the fact that it is the subject of countless advice columns in women's magazines, the lack of sexual activity and passion in a relationship is often felt as shameful. Some of this feeling, of course, is due to the fact that such an admission might suggest that one is unattractive in the eyes of one's partner. But it is more than that. Admitting one's own lack of sexual interest can be equally embarrassing, almost as if the absence of sexual desire in a relationship symbolizes inner deadness—the ultimate admission of failure. Being a desiring person, as well as a desirable one, is highly valued in our culture. The ideal of continual sexual passion is dearly held by many people, and the failure to reach it is experienced as a personal failure.

This idealization of sexual intensity burdens many people. It seems to me that almost no one today feels as though he or she is having enough sex or enough of the right kind of sex. For one couple who consulted me, the problem was that they had sex only once a week. For another, it was that they only had it once a year. And for yet another couple it was that the sex felt routine and uninventive. These deficiencies are often experienced as a private failure, disappointment, or loss.

A diminution of sexual desire is ubiquitous in long-term relationships, and, despite great individual variation, tends to be experienced by men and women equally. And why shouldn't sexual boredom be universal? How could it possibly be that the sexual intensity, idealization, and sense of delightful surprise that typifies a new relationship could remain the same over years of familiarity and intimacy, years of seeing one's partner in every physically and mentally unattractive state possible? However much new lovers may think they experience feelings of merger and total intimacy, they are actually strangers. As a stranger, each person is full of limitless possibility. With partners of many years, intimacy has eliminated their secrets, their "otherness." The possibilities are no longer endless.

Intimacy may bring a sense of safety and ease to a relationship, but it also means that partners feel less driven to please each other. New lovers, on the other hand, are singularly motivated to please each other and to present their best—not necessarily their most authentic—sides. That's what is meant by idealization. People automatically present their ideal selves to each other and don't reveal the ways that they might be depressed, anxious, angry, or defensive. Then, when couples eventually get to know each other as whole people, they encounter these darker sides, an encounter that can dampen sexual desire. Once we become intimate with someone, we're almost certain not only to see more personal characteristics that may make us feel worried or rejected, but also to care more about what we see. To the extent that we feel responsible for and aware of what ails those we love—their sensitivities, insecurities, and fears—we are less able to take their well-being for granted; in other words, the less able we are to feel comfortably ruthless. Emotional complexity begins to enter the bedroom. The result is a decline in desire in both men and women.

That pedestal on which new lovers place each other inevitably develops cracks and fissures. Such lovers increasingly encounter each other before one puts on her makeup and the other has his first cup of coffee. They more frequently see each other sick, irritable, worried, insecure, and on the toilet. His capacity to accept you with all your faults turns out to hide an underlying passivity that eventually annoys you. The strength that he showed in guiding you through emotional storms early in your relationship turns out to also reflect an emotional detachment that frustrates you. The nurturing that she seemed so ready to give you turns out to also reflect her disappointing inability to take care of herself, and the role of sexy vixen that she so frequently played early on turns out to be a burden that she quickly gives up after you're married.

As partners come to feel more sensitive to and responsible for each other, their capacity to be sexually selfish, to be ruthless, declines. In response, many people confess to me a strong desire to be "done to" by their spouses, to be relieved of the responsibility of arousing and pleasing their partners. If there is one complaint common to every relationship that I know of that is marked by sexual dissatisfaction, it is that one or both of the partners feels that the other doesn't take enough romantic initiative. While feelings of rejection often lie at the heart of these complaints, guilt and responsibility are silent culprits as well. Everyone wants to be actively wanted, not simply because they need affirmation and fear rejection but because only then can they counteract their guilt about being selfish and ruthless. The logic goes: "If you show me that you want it more than I do, then I can safely and selfishly want it as much as possible without worrying about your feelings."

For a time, the sexual enervation induced by normal familiarity may be counteracted by other experiences that accompany long-term intimacy. Familiarity may, for example, bring a sense of safety, a sense of unconditional acceptance that can facilitate sexual communication and experimentation. Couples can learn what each other likes and doesn't like and expand their sexual repertoires as a way of deepening their connection.

Further, long-term couples may often reinvigorate their sexual relationships through attempts to de-familiarize themselves with each other, for example, by donning sexier clothing, experimenting with different sexual positions, physical locations, and role-playing. It is well-known that couples often have better sex on vacation or in hotels, not only because they may be more relaxed, but because a novel environment in which they're not responsible for anything helps restore a greater interpersonal sense of novelty and difference and thus promotes ruthlessness and stimulates desire.

We all recognize the sexual appeal of variety, but we don't understand it. Variety is sought because it brings with it the psychic space necessary to experience sexual ruthlessness. By psychic space I mean a sense of mental separateness in which one's partner isn't predictable, in which neither person in a relationship can automatically assume to know what the other is feeling. In a new relationship, each partner's real internal life is relatively opaque to the other, and thus there is a tendency to invest the partner's external appearance and behavior with more glitter and excitement. To some degree, couples need to objectify each other—appreciate the external in the other—to get maximally aroused. In the course of this objectification, the other person can be viewed as sturdy and not as an object of responsibility, worry, or potential rejection. If empathy and communication is one side of the coin of sexual bliss, ruthlessness and objectification is the other.

Eventually, then, the conflict between intimacy and ruthlessness asserts itself and creates a tendency for sexual excitement to diminish. Couples return from their hotels, and their experiments with new sexual techniques become ordinary. And the growing familiarity opens the doors to the influences of each partner's families of origin, influences that inevitably have a chilling effect on a couple's ardor. It is sometimes said that when a couple is having sex, there are six people in the bed—the two partners and the parents of each of them.

The Dynamics of Sexual Chemistry— Clinical Vignettes

As soon as we descend from the level of abstract theory to the lives of real men and women, these explanations of the universality of sexual boredom break down. We are now faced with real women complaining about their husband's sexual interest. Our explanations must take into account that these men came from family backgrounds within which they developed particular pathogenic beliefs that have an impact on their sexual responses.

Jesse and Kathy

My patient, Jesse, for example, grew up feeling he was responsible for his sad mother, while his wife, Kathy, grew up worried that she could overwhelm her insecure and competitive father. Over time, these childhood beliefs created trouble in the adult bedroom. When Jesse sensed that Kathy was unsatisfied in bed, his childhood belief that he was supposed to take care of unhappy women began to surface and he felt guilty and tried harder. This made sex feel more like work to him and dampened his enthusiasm. And when Jesse seemed to be trying too hard to please her, Kathy's childhood worries about her own power to control and overwhelm men was stimulated and this inhibited her own sexual responsiveness.

In the sex life of any real couple, universal and particular forces are always interacting. As Jesse and Kathy got to know each other better and became more intimate, they became increasingly aware of each other's sensitivities and vulnerabilities. And this awareness stimulated universal processes that had a chilling effect on their sexual passion. At the same time, Jesse and Kathy also each had unique psychological conflicts. In therapy, they worked on these issues, the only ones they could control. For example, they each learned to stop worrying about and feeling responsible for the other person and instead allow themselves to become more selfish. This helped Jesse to not try so hard and Kathy to feel less responsible for Jesse's anxieties about pleasing her. As a result, they were able to improve their sex life considerably. And yet, in the end, they still tended to be overly sensitive to each other and resistant to being truly uninhibited in their sexual relationship.

Sam and Reina

Sam and Reina were another couple who consulted me about their mutual lack of sexual desire. Sam was depressed. He grew up in a family in which both his parents were depressed. Not only did he not get much in the way of emotional support from his parents, but the only way he could be a part of his family, the only way he could connect with his parents at all, was to be depressed himself. When he first met Reina, he was struck with her vitality, especially her sexual vitality. She seemed to know how to have fun and was full of playful energy. The cheerfulness Sam perceived in her was a tonic and freed him up to feel intense sexual desire. Over time, however, Sam came to see that Reina was, herself, somewhat moody, and could be periodically morose and pessimistic. This deeper awareness of his wife's moods contributed to a diminution of Sam's sexual desire. His initial impression of Reina was not wrong, but it was distorted by his idealization of her, as well as her attempts to be upbeat to please him.

Reina, on the other hand, came into the relationship feeling safe and protected by Sam's serious nature and thrilled about the extent to which, by being lively, sexy, and fun-loving, she could please him and give him something that was missing in his life. She grew up with critical parents who couldn't tolerate negative feelings or problems in their children, and she expected the same lack of acceptance from men. Initially, Sam seemed to be the type of person who would understand the shadow side of life (although she barely ventured to go there when she was with him), and this safety enabled her to feel more sexually free. Eventually Reina began to show Sam more and more of herself, including her feelings of low self-esteem. He comforted her but also began to sexually withdraw. Sensing Sam's withdrawal and experiencing it as a rejection, Reina defensively withdrew and became more self-critical and unhappy, which, of course, only perpetuated this cycle of sexual frustration.

Notwithstanding the fact that Sam and Reina's ardor was influenced by certain universal factors, their special personal inhibitions and pathogenic beliefs were significantly improved in couples therapy. Sam was helped to see, for example, that Reina's depressive states didn't represent all of who she was, and that he shouldn't mistake the part for the whole just because it superficially appeared to mirror the mood states of his parents. And Reina was helped to see that when Sam withdrew from her, it was from an irrational fear of identifying with and having to take care of her—not from a genuine wish to reject her—and that if she was more persistent and assertive in bed, Sam eventually would be convinced of her true intentions.

Laurie and Jim

As she sat in my office during our first session, Laurie nervously and repeatedly looked at her husband, Jim. Jim seemed remote and had positioned his chair so that it pointed about forty-five degrees away from Laurie. These physical postures turned out to be symbols of the underlying tension in their relationship, namely, that Laurie was anxious about their attachment and Jim was burdened by it. Laurie and Jim had been sent to me by their individual therapists for couples counseling because of a complete breakdown in their sexual relationship. Their presenting complaint seemed simple enough: Laurie had developed a medical condition that, even with treatment, resulted in decreased vaginal lubrication. In order to have sex without pain, she needed the help of an artificial lubricant of some kind and had suggested to her husband that they incorporate its application into their foreplay. Jim, however, found himself feeling terribly upset about this idea because of his belief that if Laurie's vagina was being lubricated artificially, he could never be sure if she was genuinely excited. He told her that he could tolerate it—barely—if she applied the lubricant herself, as long as he wasn't around to see it or didn't have to do it himself. He found himself repelled by the notion because of what he felt it communicated about Laurie's sexual desire. Laurie felt hurt by Jim's attitude, interpreting it as a rejection of her. She wanted Jim to desire her so much that he would *want* to do whatever it took to make sex enjoyable and easy. Eventually, they stopped having sex altogether.

The most striking thing about this situation was the extent to which Jim and Laurie completely misunderstood each other. Each person's subjective experience seemed so compellingly true that she or he was unable to grasp, much less validate, any competing version of the truth. Each had a need for reassurance that felt totally obvious, reasonable, and valid. It felt to both Jim and Laurie that to concede the other's point of view, to put themselves in each other's shoes, would be to relinquish their right to have their own emotional needs validated and met. This is a common psychological predicament in couples. Understanding is interpreted as an emotional zero-sum game—if one person's feelings are "understandable," the other person's feelings are somehow "wrong."

What didn't Jim and Laurie adequately understand? First of all, Jim was more worried than he admitted that he couldn't satisfy Laurie. In fact, his ability to satisfy a woman was at the core of his self-image. It was as if a woman's dissatisfaction completely daunted him; he felt that he had no choice but to take it to heart. Jim's father, who had a history of job failures and two previous marriages, had abandoned the family when Jim was about four years old, leaving him to be raised by a mother who was openly hostile toward men. Soon after her husband left her, Jim's mother came out as a lesbian and began publishing a radical feminist magazine that often pilloried men. Jim remembers that his mother hung a poster over their toilet that read: "Men: Can't Live with 'Em. Can't Just Kill 'Em." He said, with just a note of irony, "I had to look at this every time I peed. . . . No wonder I was confused about what it meant to be a man!" It was inevitable that Jim would develop the irrational belief that women weren't ever happy with men. At the same time, however, he came to feel that if he didn't make them happy, he was, in the words of his mother, a "pig" like his father.

For Jim to lubricate Laurie artificially would be to leave unanswered the question of whether she was *really* happy with him. The presence or absence of natural lubrication was like a verdict on how desirable he was. In his unconscious mind, he was guilty until irrefutably proven innocent. It didn't matter that Laurie reassured him otherwise. In Jim's mind, physiology spoke louder than words. For Jim to just plunge ahead and *not* worry about Laurie's "true" feelings of arousal, to have sex with her because he simply wanted to, was to risk being experienced as a selfish pig of a man. The more anxious Laurie became about his interest, or lack thereof, the more difficulty Jim had feeling desire, because her complaints and anxiety unwittingly raised the specter again of an unhappy and unsatisfied woman for whose unhappiness he was responsible.

Laurie, on the other hand, was unknowingly in the grips of her own pathogenic childhood beliefs. She had grown up with a mother who systematically belittled her and made her feel inadequate. Laurie was developmentally delayed when it came to her motor skills. She stood and moved awkwardly and had poor coordination. Her mother used to call her names like "ducky" because her toes pointed inward, and made jokes at her expense when she tripped or had trouble with her balance. Laurie complied with her mother's disparagement and felt disgusting and deficient as a person and particularly as a woman. Her problem with vaginal lubrication threatened to reinforce her feeling of being defective as a woman. For Laurie, the only way to counteract this pathogenic belief about her femininity was for Jim not only to *not mind* if she used artificial lubrication, but for him to get turned on by applying it himself during their foreplay. She interpreted his unwillingness to do so as a confirmation that her worries about herself were justified, that she was disgusting to men and inadequate as a woman. She hid this intense insecurity about her femininity behind her "reasonable" expectations that Jim stop holding an unavoidable medical condition against her.

To oversimplify the core problem: Jim experienced Laurie as an unhappy mother, and Laurie experienced Jim as a critical and rejecting one. Neither of them understood this because each one experienced himself or herself as having legitimate needs and grievances that were being ignored. Laurie couldn't understand Jim's worry because she was seeing him through the distorting lens of her own anxieties. Jim didn't understand that Laurie felt that when he gave up on trying to please her, it was a sign of his disgust for her femininity, a disgust that she secretly feared she deserved. He couldn't understand this, not only because Laurie couldn't tell him but because this wasn't Jim's experience of her problem with lubrication. Neither one could understand the other's point of view. Each of them was in the grips of the reemergence of a childhood theme that was distorting their own and each other's reactions.

Infidelity

If the decline in sexual intensity doesn't seem to be gender related, the phenomenon of infidelity certainly seems to be. Despite evidence of increasing infidelity by women, the stereotypic story of sexual betrayal and abandonment involves a middle-aged man responding to some type of midlife crisis through a romantic interlude with a sexy young woman. Such a situation seems to reveal several of the male sexual proclivities most often dreaded, hated, and, I will argue, misunderstood by both women and men.

Infidelity never occurs in a vacuum. The culturally conventional triangle described above always involves three psychologies: the man/husband, the forsaken wife, and the new nubile love interest. Sexual chemistry, good and bad, is the result of a complicated interaction between the personalities and temperaments of everyone involved, as well as reflecting the influence of social and cultural roles and expectations. The philandering husband is partly reacting to his wife, the wife to the husband, and the "other woman" to the unfaithful man. Bearing in mind the caution that there is no "one-size-fits-all" interpretation of these situations, a particular psychological story has emerged often enough in my clinical work with the people involved in these affairs to justify making generalizations about the motivations of each person involved.

The Typical Triangle

Bob and Alice had been married for fifteen years. In the beginning of their relationship, sex was frequent, experimental, and satisfying to both of them. Bob and Alice each had caretaker personalities. They were overly accommodating to the other person, a trait that they'd grown up believing was the way they were supposed to be. Both Bob and Alice were guilty about being selfish and tended to be highly sensitive to signs of displeasure in each other. They had two children to whom they were devoted. While they both worked, Alice tended to do more of the primary parenting, while

Bob made more money and worked longer hours. As a couple, they felt all the stresses of modern life described so frequently in popular magazines—financial pressures, little time for intimacy, and general psychic and physical fatigue at the end of the day.

Although both Bob and Alice had difficulty tending to their own needs, this conflict took different forms in each of them. Alice's mother had been very critical and depressed and had frequently complained about Alice's father. Alice grew up with a great deal of survivor guilt about having a happier life than her mother, particularly if that life included good sex. She told me that since she had two siblings, she had to believe that her parents had sex at least three times, but she simply couldn't imagine her mother ever enjoying it. Her parents slept in separate beds or bedrooms for much of Alice's life. Alice's mother communicated—verbally and by example—that sex wasn't something that a woman should expect to enjoy. Too guilty to reject her mother in this intimate arena, Alice complied with her and became sexually inhibited. One of the reasons she fell in love with Bob was that they initially had such great sex, temporarily freeing Alice from the repressive psychic grip of her mother. At the same time, while Alice's inhibitions bowed, they were certainly not broken. The sexual passion Alice felt with Bob conflicted with her view of what "normal" married women were supposed to feel. Her sex drive remained precarious.

Alice's father was a passive man. She was quite fond of him but also saw him as pathetic. His passivity and pathos made her feel sorry for him, and she grew up believing that she could hurt him if she was too forceful. Alice's worry about hurting her father is common among women in our culture who later feel guilty about being sexually aggressive with men. At a deeper level, Alice—like many other women—imagined that male egos were brittle and had to be protected through reassurances that their husbands were really in control. Alice always let Bob make the first move in the bedroom, and, when he didn't, she didn't push the matter further. In addition, sexually aggressive women have historically been labeled "loose." Echoes of the ancient split between images of women as mothers or whores can still be found in our collective psyches. If a man sleeps around, the social judgment might well be "boys will be boys," while if a woman does the same, she might be considered a slut.

Bob also grew up feeling worried about his mother, although his mother's suffering took the form of low energy and hypochondria. She frequently went to doctors for one complaint or another and had a medicine cabinet full of remedies that never quite solved the problem. Bob experienced her as weak and her body as fragile, a template of women that unfortunately cast a shadow on his later relationships. He often felt that he had to keep what he called his "third eye" on the woman with whom he was having sex lest he inadvertently hurt or displease her. Bob was so focused on the woman's emotional life that he expected and took little for himself. The result was a deep sense of disconnectedness.

Bob saw his father as a strong man, but one who was away from home most of the time. Bob sensed that his father's absence was motivated by a wish to escape the burden of his marriage, and Bob suspected that his father had frequent affairs while he was on the road. He didn't help or protect Bob with Bob's mother, and his absence reinforced Bob's underlying loneliness.

As with other couples, a combination of factors led to the decline of sexual intensity between Bob and Alice. First, they experienced the universal and natural tendency for sexual passion to diminish as couples become more intimate and familiar, a process that promotes positive feelings of connection and sensitivity but that also opens the doors of the mind to feelings of worry, guilt, and rejection. Second, Bob and Alice each suffered from the strain of their everyday lives—the constant work outside the home at their jobs and inside in relation to their children—and such strain and fatigue dampened their sexual ardor. And third, Alice and Bob had particular sensitivities that exaggerated the first two factors.

Bob was overly worried about hurting Alice. He needed her to demonstrate her desire more aggressively to reassure him that she (in his view, unlike most women) really wanted sensual pleasure. When she failed to initiate sex, Bob's guilt about imposing his sexual needs on an unwilling partner led him to feel even more alone. Alice, on the other hand, was worried about overwhelming Bob if she were too assertive about her sexual needs and was also struggling with a vague sense that a sexless marriage was her lot—and that of all women. Like her mother, Alice was inclined to accept life's compromises in the bedroom.

As Bob and Alice went about their busy lives, raising their children, working to raise their standard of living, fitting into the general expectations of their culture, their sex life slowly waned. Despite their intimacy, Bob and Alice began to grow more distant, although neither of them would admit it. Each person began feeling neglected, quietly (and sometimes not so quietly) complaining about being burdened and unappreciated in the relationship. Like all primary adult relationships, theirs increasingly inherited some of the distortions that each partner grew up feeling and seeing in their families of origin. Alice began to identify more with her own mother and experience Bob as weak like her father. Bob began to react to Alice as if she was like his mother—fragile, worn down by life, and unable to take care of him. They would argue more or drift into longer silences. Nothing dramatic changed, and yet everything was changing. Both Bob and Alice privately suffered from the lack of sexual intimacy but also thought it was the way that the world was supposed to be, that the expectation that two people could be intimate and sexual at the same time was one that they had resigned themselves to never realizing. At least some portion of this story can be found in many relationships today.

Then, while on a business trip, Bob met Jody, a successful artist fifteen years his junior. Bob met her in a gallery that was showing her paintings. Jody was overtly sexual in her dress and manner. She flirted with Bob. She laughed a lot and talked about how much she liked to travel. She seemed impressed with Bob's job and seemed to think that he was funny and charming.

These traits were like an aphrodisiac to Bob, and when Jody indicated her interest and availability, they began an affair. Bob felt that it was the best sex he'd ever had. He explained that the reason was that Jody seemed "up for everything and anything" and was aggressive about what she wanted. She was multiorgasmic and, in his words, was really "wild" in bed. He talked excitedly about her body, loving the youth of it, the smooth skin, the perkiness of her breasts, and even the tightness of her vagina when he was inside her. He told me, "She's so full of life. . . . She just wants to have a good time. . . . I just plug into her energy."

And they did have a good time. Bob saw her whenever he was in town and they often went out dancing, smoked pot, and had sex as often as they could. He told me that he felt like a teenager again. He was incredibly happy when he was with Jody and would get depressed when he'd come home to Alice.

Although she knew nothing of the affair, Alice sensed that Bob was shut down and felt so herself. She felt asexual over time, owing to the confluence of personal, marital, and social pressures. Bob wasn't showing interest, her (our) culture was fixated on the appeal of youth, and in her own mind she was identifying with her mother, guilty about her own sexual needs and disappointed in her husband.

Jody, of course, had her own story. She wasn't just the "other woman." She was the daughter of a mother similar to Bob's and Alice's, a mother toward whom Jody felt loyal and responsible. But in addition, Jody's father was authoritarian and cold. She felt chronically rejected by her father, and her perception was that he favored her brothers and generally devalued femininity. In the face of her guilt toward her mother and sense of shame and inferiority evoked by her father, Jody's way of finding pleasure and excitement was to seduce and excite men with her feminine beauty and prowess. If she became involved with an unavailable man, all the better. Jody believed that such a man's willingness to break a rule or take a risk was a testament to how special she really was. In so doing, Jody was unconsciously counteracting her father's disdain and momentarily overcoming the pull of her mother's unhappiness. Jody's psychology is common among women in our society who often seek out older men for the special type of protection and validation they seem to provide.

Even though the characters of Bob, Alice, and Jody have been radically oversimplified, some version of their story is common in our culture and reveals several important psychological and sexual dynamics. Over time, Bob's and Alice's growing intimacy inhibited their sexual ruthlessness; that is, their greater awareness of and concern for each other's internal states created an environment increasingly inhospitable to the kind of ruthlessness and objectification that are necessary components of intense sexual arousal. As the mutual idealizations wore off in the face of greater familiarity, the reality of the other's psychic blemishes intruded into their minds and libidos. Bob saw more and more of Alice's tendencies toward depression, and Alice became more and more sensitive to Bob's tendency to withhold emotional closeness. For each, the specters of their parents began to enter their sex life and shut it down. Paradoxically, as their relationship deepened and as their lives became increasingly intertwined, a crucial part of their connection diminished and the result was greater loneliness.

In this context, Bob's attraction to Jody is easy to understand. In Bob's mind, she was both the "anti-Alice" and the "anti-mother." She was happy and carefree, while Alice was somewhat inhibited. Jody loved sex and pleasure of all kinds, while Bob's mother was chronically suffering. Jody was aggressive, while Alice was passive. And, finally, Jody's body had the smoothness and firmness of youth—symbolizing a woman who was innocently cheerful and untroubled by life—while both Bob's mother and wife were women whose normally aging bodies bore the symbolic stamp of time, struggle, and hardship.

Bob didn't need to take care of Jody. He didn't have to work to please her. Instead, she wanted to please him, and nothing was going to be too much for her. Her youthful vivacity was like a battery into which he could plug himself, and the connection felt electric. In other words, Jody and her youthfulness were symbolic antidotes to Bob's pathogenic beliefs that women were tired, drained, and unhappy creatures with whom sex and fun were "work." She offered a connection free of responsibility. In the face of such a tonic, Bob was sexually swept away.

Such a tonic, of course, depended not only on Jody's age and personality but on the fact that their relationship was "on the side," part time, a secret alternative to the day-to-day intimacy of his marriage. In other words, the fact that Jody was "the other woman" meant that she was—for the moment—somewhat immune to the emotional baggage inherent in a primary relationship.

In Bob's unconscious sexual calculations, his wife, Alice, got a bum rap. In reality, Alice was not at all like his mother. She wasn't a weak hypochondriac. She actually would have liked Bob to be aggressive and uninhibited with her in bed but felt too guilty to say so. In Alice's mind, women weren't supposed to want a wild sex life, particularly women who were wives and mothers. She felt terribly frustrated by Bob's diminishing interest in sex and on some level experienced it as a rejection. She complied with this rebuff and allowed it to confirm her pathogenic belief that she wasn't supposed to enjoy sex and exercise her sexual power. Alice had the fantasy that if she really pushed Bob, really "jumped him," as she put it, that he'd feel overwhelmed and not be able to perform. In other words, Alice couldn't help but react to Bob as if he was pathetic like her father. Thus, while Bob's withdrawal was at least partly motivated by his worry about Alice, Alice's sexual passivity was partially motivated by the same false perception of him.

Alice, however, wasn't as available for an extramarital sexual relationship as was Bob, not only because of her lifelong personal guilt about fully expressing and enjoying her sexuality, but because women in this culture are not supposed to be eager sexual agents. Despite the gains of feminism and the growing incidence of female infidelity, women are still more constrained than men when it comes to feeling that it is their natural right to pursue and enjoy sexual pleasure, particularly if initially it is pleasure for its own sake.

When the Jodys of the world—the "other women"—enter the picture with their own set of psychological conflicts and sexual solutions, a fragile situation begins to break down. Jody was drawn to older men because she associated age with power and value. If an older man desired her, her sense of self-worth rose, her doubts about her femininity decreased, and she felt more special and protected. And if this desire was powerful enough to compel him to make a sacrifice, all the better. By counteracting her negative beliefs about herself and her value, such men made it safe for her to feel intense sexual passion. The sexual appeal of this solution, of course, is often accompanied by tremendous risk and suffering. Women like Jody do not usually "get the guy," and they wind up feeling used and rejected. In addition, the appeal of a married man carries with it an essential compromise. Jody grew up feeling that she wasn't supposed to have the whole package with a man, that is, a man who was available and loving, a man who thought her especially desirable but who was also committed to her emotionally. Bob's limitations represented exactly the type of half-baked love that Jody felt she deserved.

While Bob, Alice, and Jody are stereotypes, there are no stereotypic outcomes to their "story." Such triangles can continue for years. They can have tragic consequences, or they can motivate each party to change his or her life for the better. Although the Alices in this situation—the wives—are often the most obvious victims, all three people are caught up in a complex world of desire and pain.

Sexual Chemistry

So what can we say about sexual chemistry—or the lack thereof—in relationships? The processes by which male and female psychologies interact and create sexual chemistry reveal the fragility of sexual arousal. In all the cases presented, if a partner confirms the pathogenic beliefs that inhibit the other's sexuality, arousal diminishes. For excitement to be enhanced, a partner needs to do the opposite—namely, disprove or negate these pathogenic beliefs. Thus, when couples report that they had "instant chemistry" when they first met, we can infer that this process of negation was occurring on both sides.

Sexual attraction is simply the process by which one person's appearance and temperament helps another person unconsciously transcend the pathogenic beliefs that inhibit arousal.

Human attraction is based on the capacity of the human brain to rapidly register and interpret a huge amount of information. The fact that this process is unconscious renders sexual chemistry mysterious to those who experience it. But as we've seen, psychologists have shown that our unconscious information processing system is always active, always scanning the environment—both physical and interpersonal—looking for dangers, making judgments, guiding decision making, and interpreting meaning.

Sexual attraction, while appearing ineffable and biological, is actually based on just this sort of unconscious perception and interpretation. Since sexual arousal depends on negating the beliefs and feelings that hold it back, we subliminally perceive those qualities in others that will help us do just that, whether those qualities are physical or temperamental.

For example, if a man tends to feel guilty about and responsible for women, he might become sensitized to evidence that women he meets need caretaking. He might sense this by the way they act, look, or just by the "vibe" that they put out—something nonspecific but meaningful. A woman who acts particularly independent, appears tough and sexy, or seems to be happy, would elicit arousal in such a man, even if he is not conscious of the real meaning of what he is experiencing. A woman who looks tough might actually be quite weak, and her independence might turn out to be a defense against enormous insecurity. "At first sight," however, she subliminally provides enough evidence of what this man needs to stimulate his desire. The issue isn't what is real but what the man interprets as real, and such interpretations, as well as the perceptions and inferences upon which they are based, are occurring instantly and below the conscious level.

A man I treated, Dennis, liked, but was not sexually attracted to, his friend Isabelle. After a summer's separation, he ran into her in a class and felt a sudden attraction to her. He began to pursue her, she responded in kind, and eventually they married. Dennis came to see me two years later because he was very unhappy in his relationship, feeling intensely burdened by what he described as Isabelle's clinging dependence and constant jealousy. What had happened?

As Dennis and I reconstructed their history and explored his first moment of sexual attraction, it emerged that Isabelle looked somehow "different" on that day. Rather than the long flowing dresses that she usually wore, on that day Isabelle was wearing pants. Further, Isabelle was wearing a kerchief over her hair. Something about that "look" triggered Dennis's interest and then arousal. As Dennis thought about it, he thought that perhaps Isabelle looked more masculine than usual that day. He realized that suddenly seeing her in a more sexual way had to do with her appearing stronger and more independent. Dennis had grown up with a very sad, chronically ill mother for whom he felt intensely responsible. When he was with a woman, the guilt he felt growing up about being selfish tended to inhibit him sexually. His interpretation of Isabelle's strength, based entirely on unconscious perceptions, enabled him to become suddenly aroused.

As so often happens in relationships, the initial excitement that Dennis felt began to wear off as he got to know Isabelle better. He came to see that Isabelle's toughness was a thin veneer covering up a deep depression and sensitivity to rejection. As she responded to their intimacy by becoming more dependent and showing her unhappiness, Isabelle began to appear to Dennis more and more like his mother. He began to feel guilty about being selfish and being frequently obligated to give Isabelle reassurances that he loved her. As a result, his sexual interest began to wane.

Thus, both Dennis's sexual interest and his boredom depended on whether Isabelle disproved or confirmed his pathogenic beliefs. The initial attraction felt to him reflexive and mysterious, but was actually the result of a series of unconscious perceptions, inferences, and interpretations. The eventual alienation emerged as Dennis began to perceive other traits in Isabelle that unconsciously seemed to repeat the difficult aspects of his relationship with his mother. In my clinical experience, men may initially fall in love with the way a woman is unlike their mothers, but they stay in miserable and asexual relationships because of the way that she seems similar.

Dennis's sensitivity to signs of depression in Isabelle is frequently seen in men. The initial perception of a woman as buoyant and sexually exuberant gives way to the experience of her as dissatisfied or inhibited. Such perceptions inhibit men not only because that woman now seems like someone that they're supposed to take care of, but because in intimate contact with someone who is unhappy, the unhappiness tends to rub off—in other words, men are in danger of identifying with the woman who is dissatisfied and inhibited. That women so often tend to suppress their sexual strength and assertiveness, or experience it indirectly in the form of domination fantasies, often confirms, on an unconscious level, the pathogenic belief in men that women are weak and lack a ruthless sexual agency. The psychologies of the two sexes, then, complement each other in ways that often create problems in the bedroom.

Lolita Fantasies and the Sexual Appeal of Youth

THERE ARE MANY MEN IN OUR CULTURE like my unfaithful patient Bob; men who find themselves drawn to younger women like moths to a flame. Men who seem to be collectively caught up in an erotic obsession with nubile femininity. Who doesn't personally know either a man who has cheated on his wife with a younger woman or a woman betrayed by such a man? No one can escape this celebration of feminine youth and beauty—its idealization in films and television, its ubiquitous exploitation in advertising. It can be condemned as inherently sexist, rationalized as an unfortunate by-product of our biological urges, or simply accepted as normative social behavior. My aim here is to explain it.

Obviously, youth is celebrated in men as well as women. Ideals of youthful masculinity are powerful in both homosexual and heterosexual communities. And, as we will see when we analyze some of the more extreme manifestations of this appeal in the mind of the pedophile, the emotional forces that drive our sexual fascination with youth are not limited to one sex. Nevertheless, the traditional heterosexual Lolita story—an older man lusting after a younger woman—is so embedded in our collective experience that its exploration should be our first priority.

As we saw illustrated in Bob's story in the previous chapter, youth unconsciously symbolizes happiness. In the unconscious mind of a heterosexual man, the image of the nymphet with flawless skin and a toned body suggests a female who is unblemished by life's trials and tribulations, someone who has her life ahead of her instead of behind her, and someone with an incipient exuberance and optimism just waiting to be unleashed. Youthful feminine bodies are bodies that haven't had children or otherwise aged and don't yet show the marks of the external stresses of working or the internal stresses of depression and anxiety.

Fashion advertising frequently illustrates our idealization of youthful sexuality. A department store ad I recently saw shows a woman dressed like a little girl (although wearing high-heeled shoes) and the copy ran "letting the little girl shine through now and then." Calvin Klein ads, beginning with the famous one of Brooke Shields saying, "Nothing comes between me and my Calvins," are notorious in their evocation of Lolita-like sexuality. As a culture, we are bathed in these images, skillfully rendered in mass advertising, sculpted in the operating rooms of cosmetic surgeons, and reinforced by peer pressure every day in the lives of both young and old.

In the male imagination, these idealized images of young nymphets promise pleasure and playfulness free of obligation. They're women who seem to be willing to admire a man and learn from him. In their own fantasies, men can't fail to please such women or fail to be pleased by them. Men can connect to their female youthfulness and feel a corresponding surge of youthfulness of their own.

If, as we've seen, sexual desire arises only when special psychological inhibitions are overcome, what blocks are overcome by fantasies of nubile femininity? Simply put, in the male psyche, youthful women are *not* their mothers, or, by extension, their wives. In the male psyche, youth—and all that it symbolizes—becomes a counterweight to experiences of mothers worn down by life, scarred by an inordinate share of conflict, disappointment, and stress. Mothers, after all, have had children and have often been desexualized by their husbands and their culture. Further, as women, they have endured the various frustrations of gender inequality. The result is a tired body, psyche, and spirit. Eventually, wives inherit this role in the minds of men, who then respond by slowly losing the intensity of their sexual excitement.

What is the precise nature, then, of the threat to sexual excitement seemingly posed by mothers and wives? The danger lies in the pull a man feels to identify with his mother and mother substitutes, to feel drawn into their emotional orbit, and to shoulder feelings of responsibility for what he finds there. As we've seen, the legacy of normative male development seems to be a continual need to reinforce and reassert boundaries with the mother, defending a sense of "difference" by pushing her, and her femininity, away. The difficulty with this solution is that boys—and later, men—still want to be close to their mothers and mother substitutes, still love them and want to make them happy, and this wish is in constant tension with the need to pull away. The more intimate the relationship, the more feelings of closeness and responsibility grow and the more threatened boys and men become. And when the feminine orbit into which one is pulled seems marked by disappointment or unhappiness, the threat is even greater and sexual excitement is even more imperiled.

To the extent that boys—and later, men—have a pathogenic belief that women are hard to please, easily disappointed and critical, needy and demanding, they are vulnerable to viewing the aging process in women as a marker for these very weaknesses. In other words, the physical facts of aging are unconsciously equated with a set of burdensome emotional problems. In an intimate relationship with such women, these men will then feel a pull either to share in this weakness or to take responsibility for fixing it. Either way, sexual ardor is dampened.

It is in this context that youth becomes a fantasy remedy for what men feel ails them. A middle-aged male patient of mine recently paid a summer visit to the campus of a large university. He told me that he had an epiphany while walking around ogling the scantily clad students: "I thought to myself, this university has an especially gorgeous student body, especially the women. And then I realized that what I was seeing as beauty was largely just youth, and that while the students themselves obviously made distinctions about each other's sex appeal, I didn't. From my point of view, they were beautiful because they were young." My patient became aware of the capacity of youth to symbolize a range of attributes not intrinsically related to age.

The Case of Warren

Warren worked hard to please everyone, a trait that held him in good stead in his job as a nurse in a nursing home. He was so devoted to his patients that he would frequently spend extra unpaid time with them. "They look so sad," he'd tell me, "that I feel terrible ignoring them like everyone else does." Warren was married to an attorney and described their relationship in ways that led me to believe that his caretaker role extended to the home front. He told me that his wife was frequently overwrought and stressed out about her cases and that he would often be her sounding board. They had few friends.

Warren consulted me for help with his dissatisfaction in his marriage. He felt that his wife was excessively needy and insecure and that he felt burdened by her apparent demands for attention and caretaking. He told me that while he often felt cheated and deprived, he was too guilty to talk to his wife about it for fear that she would feel blamed and angry. Warren knew enough about psychology and therapy to know that a pattern of self-sacrifice cut across all his relationships, and that the "problem" lay somewhere inside him.

Warren had an unusual family of origin. Both parents had grown up in extremely poor and abusive families. In addition, Warren's mother had been born blind. She later married her teacher, Warren's father, whom she met when she was a student in a special school for the blind. Her husband, himself sighted, had a serious drinking problem. The combination of her disability and childhood hardship had made Warren's mother into a bitter woman who had become progressively housebound. His father, while a respected teacher, was usually depressed at home, occasionally erupting into drunken rages during which he would often hit Warren's mother. Warren told me that he never saw either parent laugh; as far as he knew, they had never enjoyed a single moment of their marriage. The primary mood in the family was one of bitter victimization. When Warren complained about anything, his parents would tell him that he had it better than they did and would go about their business as if he didn't exist. I had never heard a description of a family that was as bitter and grim as Warren's.

Understanding Warren's childhood helped him and me get a better handle on some of his central issues. Warren was a poster child for survivor guilt. He unconsciously believed that he wasn't supposed to have a better life than his parents. He felt that he was supposed to take care of others and not expect much for himself. Warren was tremendously guilty about feeling selfish in any way, and he became frequently involved in relationships in which he gave more than he received. In therapy, he soon made use of this understanding to feel a bit better and to begin to talk to his wife about what he needed from her. Initially, she became defensive and Warren retreated, but with the help of our work, he was able to get his point across to her and to encourage her to give more to him.

Warren began to feel better in every area of his marriage except one: the bedroom. Warren told me that his wife was quite inhibited in bed. After intercourse, for example, she would immediately leap out of bed to douche and return to the bedroom with a towel she would use to clean up any "mess," sometimes going so far as to change the sheets. Only then could she relax and cuddle in his arms. She liked only one position—the straight missionary. Because of his sense that his wife didn't love sex and wasn't thrilled about having it with him, Warren began to feel bored in bed. At the same time, he began to notice and fixate on his wife's physical flaws: her hips were too wide, her breasts too saggy, her derriere too flabby, her face too old, her energy level too low. He felt terribly guilty about his critical attitude and to compensate frequently told his wife how beautiful and sexy she was.

We worked on this problem for a year in therapy. We came to understand that Warren interpreted his wife's fastidious responses to sex as signs of shame and discomfort, and he took this as confirmation that she felt hurt or burdened by his sexual desire. This inference led Warren to feel not only rejected but even guiltier about his selfish wishes to focus on his own pleasure. He was unconsciously reacting to his wife as if she were his mother. Like his mother, Warren's wife appeared to him to require a high degree of attention and hard work to be satisfied, and yet, in the end, she rarely was.

Warren came to see that his wife's physical flaws represented, in his mind, her insecurity and poor self-esteem. He had unconsciously equated her emotional state with a physical one. Like his mother, Warren's wife was somehow "damaged," and he was supposed to fix her. As Warren came to understand his guilt better, he was able to be a bit more aggressive, taking charge more in the bedroom, and was surprised and delighted to find out that his wife enjoyed it. While it was a good beginning, however, both Warren and I felt that his guilt and worry about his wife, while important, weren't the whole story.

During one session, Warren was talking about his guilty fixation on his wife's physical flaws. I suggested to him that perhaps focusing on her flaws helped him feel more separate from his wife. I went on to explain that just as children often avoid someone with "cooties," Warren responded to his wife's apparent physical flaws as if they were contagious. By selectively reacting to things about her body that he didn't like, he created an experience of her as someone from whom he was repelled, someone who had something that could "rub off" on him if he got too close. Perhaps, I suggested, he created this situation to reinforce some need he had to keep his emotional and sexual distance from her. Devaluing his wife was part of an unconscious struggle to feel more separate.

Warren admitted that he did have a strong impulse to get away from his wife when he noticed her imperfections. He went on to confess that sometimes in the middle of the night, he'd sneak off to the bathroom and masturbate to pornographic pictures of nubile teenage girls.

"I sometimes even imagine that I'm with such a girl," Warren admitted with embarrassment, "when I'm having trouble keeping it up with my wife." With my encouragement, he gradually revealed more of the details of his fantasies:

> *My young lover is extremely happy and loves what I'm doing to her because it all is new to her. Her skin is smooth, almost like it's new. Everything is fresh and exciting and full of wonder. I'm introducing her to incredible sensations in her body that she's never felt before. I'm sucking her tits, and she's amazed at how big her nipples get. I teach her about my cock, and she's squealing with delight at how it feels. . . . She comes repeatedly, over and over.*

Warren was ashamed of these fantasies, not only because they seemed disloyal to his wife, but also because they made him feel like a dirty old man. Despite the fact that Warren, like most men in our culture, had been drenched with erotic images of teenage girls—whether in the form of fashion ads or television characters—he still felt that his fantasies were deviant. He worried that even his own therapist would be judgmental and moralistic and thus had not revealed these thoughts until he felt safe enough to do so. Still, Warren repeatedly reassured me that he would never dream of acting on his fantasies, although he admitted that he felt addicted to the images.

"The girl is perfectly designed to get you excited," I told him. "She's the opposite of your wife, whom you see as flawed. It's OK to be close to her because you can connect with her newness, her enthusiasm, her sense that her life is all ahead of her. It picks you up, like tapping into an energy source, rather than pulling you down." Warren agreed and added, "It's also that I can do no wrong."

Warren could get turned on by his fantasy nymphet because it was safe to do so. The psychological danger with his wife stemmed not only from his guilt but also from his identification with her. He loved his wife and felt emotionally connected to her. This made him enormously sensitive to anything negative, troubled, or emotionally out of balance in her. This process, which we have seen is common in couples, was tremendously exaggerated in this case because Warren had been so impaled by his parents' misery and bitterness. He was exquisitely sensitive to a woman's displeasure and had to resort to rather extreme measures to get any distance from her. He couldn't easily mentally separate himself from his wife and maintain his own positive feelings without then feeling guilty and totally disconnected from her. We came to understand that Warren struggled to maintain his boundaries in whatever way he could, even if that meant exaggerating his wife's physical flaws and unconsciously using his feelings of disgust to rationalize his turning away from her.

The image of youthful, spontaneous sexuality solved Warren's problem of identification. In fantasy, Warren could share the girl's upbeat sense of wonder and excitement rather than her human frailty. The teenage girl precisely counteracted the image of a grim and stressed mother or wife—a woman beaten down by the world—images that were symbolically represented by the small physical changes in his wife that Warren chose to focus on and be repelled by. In the pornographic images he created, Warren found the following unconscious equation: youthfulness = unblemished = spontaneous = optimistic = excited. With such a partner, Warren's own Lolita, he could borrow from her energy bank and overcome the danger of identifying with a grim wife or mother.

So what happened to Warren and his fixation on youth? The answer is that Warren never relinquished this particular fascination. He still masturbated to images of young women and admitted that he used such images sometimes when he was having sex with his wife. What did occur, however, was that Warren became more accepting of his wife. He found ways to get around his instinctive critical response to her physical flaws so that their sex life improved. As he understood more of the reasons behind his obsession with youthful femininity, he was able to let himself get emotionally closer to his wife, to become more accepting and tolerant of her "flaws."

In a man's efforts to negotiate a balance between separateness and connection, masculinity and relatedness, independence and intimacy, he is vulnerable to leaning too far either way. There is a universal human tendency to identify with people we need or love, to become like the objects of our desire. For men, becoming like a woman—particularly a woman with real needs and problems—is especially threatening because of the special guilt that men feel about satisfying women and the special way that masculinity is grounded in a rejection of femininity. When such a threat is activated in intimate relationships with women, as it must be, the stage is set for an idealization of youthful femininity. Such femininity symbolically speaks to men's fears of getting too close to real women, in other words, women their own age. It says: "Don't worry about me. You don't have to give anything up to be close to me, don't have to take care of me. I won't bring you down. Instead, I'll lift you up with my energy, my optimism, my happiness."

The Pedophile

Some people argue that men's sexual fixation on youth in contemporary society opens the psychic door to an increased prevalence of frank pedophilia. And the pedophile is so despised today that exploring his internal psychology seems, to some, perilously close to giving this monster a "pass." I disagree. In my view, it is imperative that we maintain a healthy outrage at the terrible harm that pedophiles cause and still try to understand these men as human and not alien beasts. Pedophiles are not a different species. It behooves us to understand the impulse to have sex with children while morally condemning this impulse in all of its manifestations. It is crucial to do so both to devise strategies for helping these men and to better protect the children they threaten.

The psychological damage of child sexual abuse can be grievous. As a psychotherapist who has treated dozens of victims of such abuse, I have seen firsthand how invaded, exploited, confused, and frightened a child feels in response to molestation, and I have repeatedly witnessed its long-term psychological consequences for relationships, sexuality, and self-esteem. Pedophilia is especially destructive because it compromises the child's relationship to reality itself. When someone who is supposed to protect you hurts you instead, or hurts you in the guise of loving you, your very sense of reality can become damaged. Victims of sexual abuse often blame themselves for their own victimization, and may come to feel that love itself is dangerous. The psychoanalyst Leonard Shengold has described traumas like this as "soul murders."

Our increased awareness of and sensitivity to the pain of the victims of sexual abuse represent a victory for feminist, child advocacy, and victims-rights groups, who have been arguing for many years that the violence done by men to both women and children has been whitewashed and denied in our society. The recent sexual scandals in the Catholic Church are one example of the fruits of this victory. Pedophile priests were historically protected by their bishops through flat denials, attacks on or payoffs to the victims, or by transferring the perpetrators to other churches or to the care of mental health professionals. Because of our heightened awareness of the psychological harm of pedophilia, the doors of defensiveness and denial have been smashed in diocese after diocese, priests have been punished, and restitution has begun to be made to the victims.

Is it possible to maintain a healthy outrage at the terrible harm that the pedophile causes and still try to understand these men as human and not alien beasts? Pedophiles are not a different species. If a sexual attraction to children is to be understood as obeying the same secret logic as all sexual desires, it must somehow represent an attempt to negate or overcome a pathogenic belief. And thus, the argument that our cultural celebration of nubile sexuality indirectly sanctions pedophilia contains an important insight: the pedophile is, in fact, enacting a fantasy that is distantly related to one held by many men at large—namely, the sexual appeal of youth—and, therefore, the underlying issues are related as well. The sexual appeal of youth derives from the fantasy that youth is equated with happiness and optimism and, therefore, a connection with a young woman (or man) promises to counteract feelings of depression, rejection, and guilt. As we've seen, youthful sexuality is an antidote to the inhibitory effects of the default images that many men have of women, depictions toward which men feel guilt and from which they fear contamination.

For the pedophile, the beauty and appeal of children is somewhat similar, lying as it does in the innocence and smallness of the objects of his desire. He experiences his child victims as uncontaminated by life and unthreatening. Adult sexuality, in contrast, is experienced by the abuser as threatening because of his fears that he can never please adults and that adults will judge, criticize, and dominate him. When the pedophile sexually connects with a child, whether a boy or girl, he feels as if he has plugged in to the child's youthful and exuberant energy. And he is in control rather than being controlled.

In addition, the male pedophile has often grown up desperately missing a strong father, or else has been abused by a father or father substitute. He may well have the fantasy that sexual contact with a child is a loving exchange, while simultaneously knowing that it is harmful. It is difficult for those of us who find this behavior repugnant to understand that it could possibly be construed, even by the perpetrator, in a positive light. But it is often the case that in the fantasy of mutuality that the pedophile constructs to justify his actions, he is providing his child victims with a connection to the strong and loving father that the child, and vicariously the pedophile, never had.

Further, men who molest children were often molested themselves as children. Such traumatic experiences have at least two consequences. First, since the child's helplessness was so overwhelming, he grows up and feels safe only when he turns the table on someone—in this case a child—and repeats the abusive relationship from a position of authority and power. Second, the pedophile may grow up with the pathogenic belief that inappropriate sexual contact is a sign of love and that even such tortured connections are better than none at all.

Priests who molest boys offer a good example of many of these dynamics. In my clinical experience of treating priests, some of whom had had sexual contact with children, a common story emerged. Many of these men grew up in a family in which the mother invested in them all of the ambition, esteem, and dreams that she sacrificed in her own life, creating an intense bond of obligation and guilt that her son fruitlessly tried to escape and later transferred onto the church. The priest-to-be, often his mother's favorite, was burdened with the unconscious knowledge that it was his responsibility to redeem his mother and her life of sacrifice. The father in these families was generally excluded (or excluded himself) from this intense symbiotic relationship. Meanwhile, the son developed the pathogenic belief that masculinity and mature independence would threaten his mother and her need for vicarious success, and so he devalued those traits in himself.

The burden of these unconscious feelings of obligation is a high price to pay, even if sublimated into a vocational choice of high status and reward. Not only is sex forbidden, but for such a priest, real women are dangerous because they evoke the image of the mother on whose altar he had to sacrifice his autonomy and masculinity. Further, he has intuited, often correctly, that his mother couldn't tolerate being displaced by another woman. Boys, however, are safe sexual choices because they are the precise opposite. Unlike women, these boys demand nothing in exchange for their adoration. With a boy, the priest is powerful and not helpless.

All these characteristics provide the foundation for the priest's erotic interest. In addition, the priest gets to give to the boy what he himself never had, namely, the attention and love of a strong father figure. These priests and boys reenact, over and over, a ritual in which a father is giving to a son and vice versa, with no woman around to interfere by demanding attention and caretaking. In these cases, sex with boys is exciting because it disconfirms the priest's powerful pathogenic beliefs that he is supposed to be the missing part of his mother's life and that masculinity and autonomy are harmful.

These explanations don't begin to exhaust the reasons that men molest. To a great extent, these reasons are highly particular to the individual perpetrator. There are, for example, great variations in how much aggression is necessary in these interactions, the preferred age and sex of the victim, and how far the sexual violation is carried. But regardless of these variations, the sexuality of the pedophile has the same basic structure as the sexuality of the rest of us—namely, that psychic dangers are being skirted, pathogenic beliefs disconfirmed, and inhibitions overcome. The dangers might be greater and the culture of the priesthood and the church might have encouraged the use of children as a means of overcoming inhibitions. But the pedophile isn't an alien or an empty vessel into which evil has been poured. He grew up in a family in which he developed painful and terrifying feelings that he attempts to overcome every time he sexually acts out with a child.

Understanding isn't the same as excusing. But to decide on the proper balance of treatment and punishment we have to understand the motivations of the perpetrator and the harm done to the victim. We cannot do this if we make the pedophile into a "thing" without a mind, childhood, or motivation that other human beings can understand. The model of sexuality that we have been using to understand men in general is well suited to this task because it presumes that people are primarily motivated by healthy desires but can experience the satisfaction of these desires as so dangerous that they have to go to extraordinary—and sometimes pathological—lengths to do so.

Sexual Aggression and Pornography— Myths and Realities

THERE IS HARDLY A WOMAN ALIVE who hasn't felt herself to be a victim of a sexually aggressive man. From overt sexual violence to subtly intrusive flirtation, male aggression is an unfortunate fact of life for most women. However, the meaning of this fact is frequently misunderstood by both sexes. Women *and* men often fail to distinguish between male sexual behavior consciously intended to hurt women and behavior intended to overcome an irrational fear of hurting women. Such a failure leads to unnecessary resentment and guilt in both genders.

I've treated men with both types of aggression, and their underlying psychological dynamics are completely different. There are obviously men—rapists, for example—whose sexual arousal depends on the fear and suffering of their female victims. Most men, however, would find such responses to be horrifying and incompatible with sexual excitement. These same men, however, might be aroused by a rape fantasy in which a woman is being dominated and somehow coerced into having sex, only to become eventually aroused by the experience. In both cases, force is crucial to arousal. What is the psychological difference?

In the case of actual rape and sexual violence, the male perpetrators hate women and derive sexual satisfaction from making and watching women feel helpless, frightened, and degraded. The source of this satisfaction is very specific and clear. Such arousal emerges because the sexually violent man feels psychologically safe and triumphant only when he's hurting or frightening women. The safety in rendering a woman hurt and helpless results from the perpetrator's unconscious calculus that it is she who is helplessly suffering and not he. An exploration of the childhood backgrounds of men who enjoy hurting women invariably turns up a record of sadistic abuse and memories of being made to feel helpless, frightened, and degraded. Sometimes the perpetrator was the mother, other times the father. Either way, such boys grew up in cruel environments that they internalize and later act out in their cruelty toward women.

Psychologists call this phenomenon *identification with the aggressor,* a common psychic mechanism by which people do unto others what was done unto them. Helplessness is usually a constituent of childhood trauma—after all, the child can't possibly resist the authority of his parents—and helplessness is one of the most toxic of human experiences. To some degree we all unconsciously recognize that to have a semblance of power and control, it is safer to be a victimizer than a victim. Identification with the aggressor, then, is a universal response to helplessness, fear, and suffering.

This psychological reflex in which we do unto others what was once done unto us probably lies behind most of the harmful things that we do to others, or behaviors we saw in our parents and vowed not to repeat. In its more dramatic forms, it probably lies behind the tendency of prisoners to adopt the attitudes of their jailers, the phenomenon of "hazing" in fraternities in which older members torment younger ones, and the widely recognized fact that child abusers were once, themselves, abused.

In the present context, however, it forms one of the motivations for sexual violence. If, as a child, a man was overwhelmed, devalued, and perhaps even terrorized—especially if such traumas had a sexual dimension—then this will not only generate a great deal of rage, but also create a pressure to turn the tables on others who are perceived as helpless, for instance, women, and inflict the same injuries that were once inflicted on him.

Psychotherapists see this process every day in their consulting rooms. Victimizing others via traits and behaviors that once victimized us is a common human tendency. It is a tendency that is evoked in the famous quote by Lyndon Johnson who, when asked why he didn't fire J. Edgar Hoover, replied: "I'd rather have him inside the tent pissing out, than outside the tent pissing in." Growing up dependent on our parents for survival and emotionally compliant with their authority, we naturally tend to become what we fear, taking inside our "tent"—our selves—the forces that hurt and make us powerless and then directing this abuse outward.

It is often said that rape is about power and not sex. This axiom, however, can sometimes be misleading. For the victims, the crime obviously has nothing to do with passion and everything to do with power and degradation. But for the rapist, the act is about both sex and power—power because the act depends totally on the helplessness of the victim, and sex because the rapist usually is sexually aroused by this helplessness. That the rapist requires his victim to be helpless to get excited doesn't necessarily make power his primary aim, but it may make power a means to a sexual end. Even homosexual rape in prison is pleasurable to the dominant man because it reminds him and others that he is powerful in a context in which he is objectively helpless.

In everyday social life, the rapist is always animated by fear of and hatred toward women, even when he is not enacting it, just as violent bullies are always looking for opportunities to terrorize someone weaker than themselves to reverse the constant threat of helplessness and humiliation that they themselves feel. Similarly, the aims of the rapist are simultaneously pleasure, safety, and revenge.

Men who enjoy fantasies of rape or forcible sex, however, are rarely rapists or even potential rapists. Their motivations are different, their psychological makeups of a different order than those of men whose pleasure depends on the pain and helplessness of women. They may be drawn to particular types of pornography featuring fantasies about forcing a woman to submit sexually, or they may prefer scenarios in which positions of dominance and submission are acted out. But in all these cases a crucial ingredient is that the woman becomes sexually aroused. Without this ingredient, most of the enactments of power, domination, and degradation commonly seen in heterosexual pornography and the private fantasy lives of heterosexual men would completely lose their appeal. The reason for this is simple but frequently misunderstood: *In the unconscious minds of men, the perception that a woman feels pleasure in a sexual scenario—any sexual scenario, regardless of the extent of its violence—is taken as definitive evidence that she is not hurt.*

The fantasy that women enjoy being forced to have sex finds expression in two very different situations that are often conflated. One expression of such a fantasy is the familiar "rape myth" used by men to justify sexual harassment and violence (e.g., "she wanted it"). This often appears as a post hoc rationalization for the hostile and predatory sexual behavior of men whose excitement actually depends on the helplessness and humiliation of women, not their pleasure. The other expression of the fantasy that women enjoy the experience of force in sex can be found, I believe, in the minds of most men and most heterosexual pornography. In this latter situation, the belief that women enjoy being forced is used to overcome irrational and unhealthy feelings of guilt and responsibility toward women. Without some palpable perception of the woman's pleasure, arousal for these men is impossible. Most men are so guilty about their desires to be ruthless, powerful, and dominant that they create a fantasy in which women enjoy—rather than suffer from—being dominated. And while real rape itself intrinsically involves hatred and domination, wishes to forcefully dominate and be powerful are not intrinsically misogynistic. For many men, the myth that women like to be sexually forced, a story featured in masturbatory or pornographic fantasies, is a defense against irrational feelings of guilt about hurting women, not a direct expression of a wish to do so. Rape fantasies are not about sexual violence but sexual ruthlessness.

Sexual ruthlessness is not the same as sexual violence. The former involves a wish to be selfish, the latter a wish to hurt and devalue. Most actual rapists enjoy the helplessness and pain of their victims; in fact, it's the precondition for their arousal. A man expressing sexual ruthlessness or becoming aroused by a pornographic depiction of a rape fantasy, on the other hand, doesn't want to hurt women but to take for granted that the women are strong and happy so that he can be sexually selfish without worry or guilt. In fact, most men are instantly turned off when they perceive or expect that their female partners are actually unhappy. These men want to be strong, phallic, or even dominant and have their partners enjoy and not feel threatened by it.

Male fantasies of sexual force or rape, then, in which the female victim eventually enjoys herself are imaginative attempts to disprove or negate the pathogenic belief that women are weak, unhappy, and demanding. Further, complementary fantasies are often found in the erotic imaginations of many women. No one who has read Nancy Friday's compendia of women's sexual fantasies or been titillated by romance novels or had the opportunity I've had to listen to women in therapy describe their innermost erotic desires would doubt that women, too, enjoy scenarios of sexual domination, force, and violation.

The Psychology of Pornography

The theme of rape or sexual force is but one scenario depicted in heterosexual pornography. The psychoanalyst Robert Stoller once remarked that there are as many forms of porn as there are sexual fantasies. The Internet—with its anonymity and ubiquitous availability—has made this equation even more apparent. The number and types of sexual fantasies now available for consumption online are so vast that it's fair to say they are limited only by the human imagination.

Despite the fact that depictions of sexuality in mainstream media increasingly appear pornographic, and despite its easy availability to people of all ages, pornography continues to vex both men and women today. While some forms of porn are now pitched to women and couples, it remains primarily the province of men. As such, it reflects and speaks to psychological desires and issues that are peculiar to men. While my clinical practice has included dozens of women troubled by their partners' interest in pornography, I've never treated a man who came in complaining of a similar interest in his wife.

The use and meaning of pornography highlights the ambiguities inherent in male sexual fantasy. A man's pleasure in using pornography is, at once, real and not real. It is real in the sense that he is *doing* and experiencing something concrete and palpable, but it is not real in the sense that the *meaning* of his action lies entirely in his imagination. It is real in the sense that he may actually prefer using porn to masturbate rather than have sex with his partner, but it is unreal in the sense that he knows all the while that porn is a fantastic—and momentary—escape. Such ambiguity is a source of tremendous misunderstanding and conflict between men and women today.

Women are often upset by their male partners' interest in pornography. Such reactions have certainly found expression in a vast feminist literature on the subject over the last thirty years. And with the rise of interest in online porn, a recent rash of popular books have appeared with a similar antipornography agenda (e.g., *Pornified, Getting Off, Porn Generation*, etc.). Women have many complaints about pornography, often finding the objectification inherent in it to be offensive. However, in my clinical experience, among the many objections women raise to a man's use of pornography, the two that are most passionate are (1) that men want their real-life partners to look like porn stars and do what porn stars do, and (2) that pornography reflects the male wish that women put their bodies and sexuality at the service of men. Both assumptions make women feel devalued.

Here we see the tremendous gulf between the sexual experiences of men and women. In my view, women confuse the effects of pornography with its psychological intention. It is true that porn caricatures the cultural burden women feel to remain young, thin, firm, and sexy. But the attraction to men of such images of "perfect" women putting themselves at the service of men is *not* because it shores up flagging male egos. For men, the women in pornography are not surrendering themselves but fulfilling themselves in the act of fulfilling men, a *fantasy* that counteracts the chronic guilt and responsibility that men feel toward the opposite sex. "Perfect" women are, symbolically, happy women. That such women appear to be consumed with desire for men is an unconscious marker that they are enjoying their lives in ways that free men up to enjoy their own. Women often interpret the plots, themes, and fetishes in pornography as reflecting a patriarchal belief in male superiority, while men are attracted to these representations because they counteract the idea that women feel inferior or insecure about their sexuality and, as a result, don't enjoy pleasing men.

These misunderstandings are common. Women often feel that, deep down, men want them to act like porn starlets, and thus they react with feelings of inadequacy and resentment. Such inferences about men are usually wrong. Men want women to be what porn starlets symbolically represent, namely, women who are strong and healthy enough to love sexual pleasure and love giving it to men. Both women and men often confuse the hidden theme of pornography with the manifest plot.

Objectification is a necessary component of sexual ruthlessness—for both sexes. In and of itself, it is not pathological, nor is its use limited to men. In fact, if by objectification we mean the process of rendering a three-dimensional human being into a two-dimensional image or thing, then most sexual fantasies inevitably involve some type of objectification. For example, consider two sexual fantasies that appear to be radically different and morally incomparable—a man aroused by an X-rated movie depicting a group of frat boys taking turns having sex with the prom queen, and a woman aroused by the fantasy of a tall, dark, handsome stranger sweeping her off her feet and "having his way" with her. In both cases, the sexual fantasy object of desire is not a real person. While the prom queen is obviously a figment of the man's imagination, so too the handsome stranger is not a complex person in his own right. In both cases the fantasizer reduces a real person to an abstraction. In both cases that abstraction is arousing because it temporarily overcomes some type of pathogenic belief or inhibition: the prom queen aroused by her gang bang counteracts the man's guilt about hurting women, and the tall dark stranger negates the woman's exaggerated feelings of responsibility and rejection.

My point here, however, is not that these two situations are identical in all ways but that both fantasies employ objectification and that this is a normal and necessary part of sexual fantasies in both sexes. The difference between fantasies that have a violent plot and those that don't is more relevant to the observer than to the person doing the fantasizing. A woman who vicariously puts herself in the position of the prom queen would feel degraded and humiliated—and not aroused at all—while a man who found himself put in the position of the tall, dark, handsome stranger might feel burdened, if also somewhat flattered. One scenario might arouse an observer while another may be threatening. The point is this: *The response of the observer is not a good indicator of the subjective meaning of the fantasy.*

Not bound by the constraints of reality, our imaginations can create or selectively exaggerate the particular elements in a fantasy that most efficiently overcome the blocks to sexual arousal. If a woman needs reassurance that she is not defective, she may exaggerate the degree of adoration she gets in her fantasy (for instance, a woman's fantasy that she is a queen with her suitors, or a stripper driving her male audience wild with desire) or be aroused by stories and movies that depict that kind of adoration. If she needs to disconfirm a pathogenic belief that she is responsible for men and can easily hurt them, she might get excited by images of "bad boys," or choose them as her sexual partners. Either way, she is objectifying these men, in the sense that "bad boys" are merely an image and cannot be an accurate representation of emotional reality. And yet it isn't their reality that turns the woman on; it's the unconscious use of them as an objectified image.

Likewise, most heterosexual pornography and many of the private sexual fantasies of men depict women who seem to exist primarily to sexually service men and derive tremendous pleasure themselves from the effort to do so. Such fantasy women arouse men not because they appeal to misogyny but because they counteract certain common pathogenic beliefs, for example, that women don't enjoy sex, don't enjoy pleasing men, and easily feel disappointed or hurt by men pursuing their own interests. While real women would probably feel devalued by the notion that their primary role is to service men, the women in these movies do not, and that is the key to their effect. Rather than devalued, these pornographic women are depicted as being happy, and it is their happiness—and their pleasure in making men happy—that is arousing to the male viewers.

Pornography: Chicken or Egg?

This assertion that men get turned on more by images of happy women than devalued ones is certainly a controversial one. In fact, it would be decried by a generation of feminist scholars and researchers who have made powerful claims that, like television violence, exposure to pornography shapes attitudes in ways that lead men to act badly toward women. How could it be, they argue, that exposing men to the distorted sexual norms, body types, and attitudes in porn wouldn't eventually create similar preferences in real men in the real world?

These arguments rest on the assumption that we learn who, what, and how to desire sexually through a process of socialization. According to this view, men develop sexual interests that involve negative attitudes toward women through modeling the behavior they typically see in their families, peer groups, and media. Men see that women are devalued and sexually objectified and so devalue and sexually objectify women. Women see that men prefer femininity over intelligence and so downplay their intelligence and learn to flirt in feminine—that is, culturally acceptable—ways.

The assumption that people form their desires through imitation is wrong. Our minds are not blank slates upon which the social world inscribes our beliefs and feelings. If one believes that our minds actively interpret and even sometimes distort what we see and experience, and do not simply passively reflect it, then the imitation model of sexual learning is unpersuasive. Why is it, for example, that some men raised in families and communities with rigid and patriarchal sex roles do not repeat these patterns? Why do some, even many, women raised in patriarchal families reject a subordinate role completely, in and out of the bedroom? The complicating factor that gets between the world and our behavior, between society and our true selves, is the unconscious mind.

Given the importance of the unconscious mind, assessing the effects of media exposure on someone's sexual desires and beliefs is extraordinarily difficult. How could we possibly judge whether someone's sado-masochistic preferences were created or even strengthened by chronic exposure to similar media images, and differentiate between the influence of advertising and that of a person's experience in a family or peer group? Researchers can't possibly control for such variables. We might assume that it makes some contribution, but it seems to me impossible to determine how much.

The one area in which some psychological researchers have claimed partial success in establishing an empirical relationship between exposure to erotic images and stories and attitudes toward women is pornography. In the late 1970s and 1980s, social psychologists studied the effects of pornography on the attitudes that men have toward women and on the forms and aims of their sexual desires. They wanted to know if such experiences make it more likely that men will sexually devalue and otherwise mistreat women and if they increase the likelihood of rape or other forms of sexual violence.

Such research proliferated in response to a tumultuous political environment. Pornography was seen by many feminists as one of the bedrocks on which sexism stood in our society. To others, the various attempts to censor it made pornography into a symbol of First Amendment rights. And to still others, including some feminists, porn was a radical protest against sexual conformity and repression.

My own clinical experience has made it clear to me that we can learn a great deal about a man's psychic makeup from looking at the sexual fantasies enacted in the pornography that he prefers. Still, the question remains: is pornography a cause or an effect?

Unfortunately, because the question has as much to do with politics as science, the answer is: it depends on whom you ask. The ultraconservative Meese Commission, set up in 1986 to publicize a new attack on pornography and obscenity, concluded that exposure to sexually violent materials increased not only sexual violence but aggressive behavior in general toward women. Many experts, however, including some of the very researchers that the commission relied on to support their official findings, publicly denounced these findings and argued that the data did not support these conclusions.

The empirical studies on the psychological effects of pornography on men have yielded conflicting results, in part because of the difficulty of generalizing from the laboratory to the real world. Almost all of these studies were done in conditions contrived in a psychological laboratory, usually on a college campus, conditions that were radically different from the subjects' natural everyday environments. For example, researchers devised ways to test whether, under controlled experimental conditions, exposure to pornography increased a man's disposition to use force with a woman during sex. Since such outcomes can't be observed in the laboratory, indirect measures of such a disposition had to be developed. Verbal reports were used. Often, the male subjects in these situations *said* that they would, indeed, be more inclined to use sexual force. In addition to the potential mistake of taking a subject's verbal reports of his inclinations at face value, to conclude that in that subject's real life, pornography increases his desire to force a woman to have sex, or even the likelihood that he will, would be to ignore the many mitigating factors that exist in his social life that would influence such an outcome and that can't be controlled for in a laboratory. What if he is in a relationship with a woman he adores and seeks always to please—would his inhibitions against rape be lowered at all? Do particular family or childhood experiences potentiate or mitigate the alleged increase in sexual aggression? The fact that these questions are impossible to answer limits what is called the "ecological validity" of these experiments, that is, the validity of concluding that a particular result observed under experimental conditions can be generalized to actual social life.

Furthermore, even in these flawed experiments when researchers exposed some subjects to movies that were pornographic but nonviolent (defined as sexually explicit but without any depictions of the overt use of force or violence, for example, *Debbie Does Dallas*) and others to purely violent, but not pornographically sexual, movies (for example, *Texas Chain-Saw Massacre*), it was only the latter violent films that had an effect, not the nonviolent sexual ones. If there was any effect at all, it was attributable to violence, not sex. Thus, these studies not only had the problem of generalizing from the laboratory to the real world, but also one of defining and separating out the actual elements in pornography that caused the observed effects.

Finally, pornography researchers usually take the self-report of their male subjects at face value. If, for example, following exposure to pornography depicting rape, a male subject tells the experimenter that he was aroused by this depiction, or that he would likely rape a woman if he could be guaranteed that there would be no repercussions, the experimenters usually take these responses to be accurate accounts of their subjects' true desires to degrade and hurt women.

The problem is that saying it doesn't make it so. In my reading of this research, both researcher and subject often conflate the distinction between fantasy and reality. It is true that many men have rape fantasies, as do many women. For both sexes, the fantasy rapes usually end with the woman becoming aroused and freely participating. Researchers wouldn't assume, of course, that women want to actually enact their fantasies about being physically overpowered by a man. Yet when men get aroused by rape depictions or confess a desire to enact one, researchers don't question whether the male respondents are expressing an authentic wish to have sex with a woman against her will or are instead expressing a fantasy that has other meanings. What many sex researchers fail to appreciate is the central role of guilt in the male psyche. One of the reasons that the myth that women want or invite rape exists at all is because, on the whole, most men are so guilty about their desires to be ruthless, powerful, and dominant that they create a fantasy in which women enjoy being dominated. If such fantasies are not being used as an excuse to rape or as a post hoc justification for a past rape, such desires are not inherently misogynistic, since their primary unconscious aim is not to hurt or degrade women.

Underneath it all, the psychological problem for these men—most men, I believe—involves exaggerated feelings of guilt and responsibility that prevent them from feeling sexually free, powerful, and uninhibited. Male fantasies of rape in which the woman eventually enjoys herself are imaginative attempts to disprove or negate the pathogenic belief, so common in men, that women are weak, envious, and demanding.

Thus, when a male subject in a pornography experiment says that he was aroused by a rape scenario, his arousal isn't necessarily an endorsement of misogynist violence, but is more likely the excitement that is unleashed when his chronic fears of hurting women are temporarily overcome by the presence of arousal in the woman depicted in the scenario. Most of these subjects, in my view, would instantly lose their erection if, while enacting such a scenario with a real woman, she were to indicate that she was actually being injured or traumatized. And yet, because the psychological logic behind sexual fantasies is unconscious and misunderstood, researchers and lay people alike take the admission of arousal over rape scenarios as the objective and enduring truth of a man's misogyny and wish to rape.

A great deal has been written about the psychic and physical violence done to women in the sex industry. Their victimization by producers, directors, and male costars is well-known. In fact such victimization is often the adult version of the sexual abuse of their own childhoods. The fact that so many thousands of women are hurt through their involvement in the industry—their "free choice" notwithstanding—is not, unfortunately, relevant to the question of what pornography means to men. The fact that women are abused in the making of porn does not mean that male consumers of porn are aroused by abusing women. Most male consumers of pornography are aroused by representations of female sexual arousal, not female abuse. The distinction here is crucial if our project is to understand the appeal of pornography to the male viewer.

There are, however, exceptions to every rule. And the psychological meanings of pornography to its consumers cannot be reduced simply to an attempt by men to counteract feelings of guilt and loneliness. Men are driven by other desires, and as a result pornography has other meanings. There are times when the consumption if not the enactment of sexual fantasies in pornography can cause great harm to women, times when a man's use of pornography reinforces his avoidance of intimacy. In these cases, the man is so terribly afraid of his own dependency needs, so worried about falling under the dominion of a woman, that he must disconnect entirely from her.

One way of disconnecting, while enjoying a measure of pleasure, is through certain types of pornography and sexual fantasy that depict scenarios of extreme degradation of women. The unconscious logic is something like: "I'm in total charge and unaffected by a woman's power." In these cases, a man may not want to actually do the things depicted on the screen, but the fantasies themselves keep him from confronting his real problem, namely, his fear of submitting to women. The partners of such men often feel rejected, even during sex, and don't quite know why. In fact, they are sensing the man's intention, which is to keep her out, away from him, and in her "place."

I recently treated a woman, Julia, who had been married for ten years to John, a man whom she described as gentle and a bit passive. She had been complaining because John had been uninterested in sex for a long time. In addition, Julia had increasingly borne the brunt of John's irritability in their nonsexual life together. The few times that they had had sex, John seemed emotionally distant. Upon returning home unexpectedly one day, Julia found John masturbating to a pornographic video called *Gangbang Girl*. On being confronted, he admitted that he was sexually attracted to younger women and preferred porn in which girls were being degraded in some way, although they always also enjoyed the process. He admitted that he had been thinking of pornographic scenes while having sex with Julia, an admission that made sense of his emotional disconnectedness. Julia was devastated.

The point of this vignette is to show one way that pornography can be destructive, even if the deepest intention of the man using it is not primarily hostile. John was someone who actually felt very resentful toward women because he feared their power over him, but he suppressed his hostility and became passive instead of directly expressing his feelings. Both his fear and hostility toward women made normal sex impossible, but pornographic depictions of women enjoying his aggression rather than feeling devalued by it turned him on. He couldn't talk about this with Julia and, instead, simply acted it out. He was either uninterested in sex or had to use an extreme sado-masochistic fantasy to perform with her. Whatever John's deepest motives might be, the net result of this conflict was that Julia was the object of his hostility during the day and was bypassed entirely at night.

CHAPTER 7

From Morality to Meaning: Changing Male Sexuality

F MEN ARE IN TREATMENT with me long enough, they will eventually allude to some problem in their sex lives. One patient might complain that he has no desire for his wife and wonders if he should leave her, while another tells me that his lack of interest is frustrating his wife so much that she is threatening to leave him. Another patient will confide in me that he worries he's abnormal because he can get aroused only by being dominated by a women, while still another might confess that he compulsively frequents strip joints and sexually oriented chat rooms on the Internet and knows that this behavior makes having an intimate relationship more difficult.

I hear about the sexual difficulties of men from my women patients as well. Typical complaints include "He doesn't seem connected to me while we're having sex," or "He rarely wants to have it and, when he does, doesn't seem open to learning about how to please me," or "When we're out in public he gets whiplash checking out younger women," or "I recently found a porn stash in his closet."

Nevertheless, given the great emotional suffering often engendered by conflicts about sexuality, it is striking to me the lengths to which patients of both sexes go to avoid talking about it. While sexual conflicts are occasionally at the top of the list of patients' problems when they enter therapy, these issue generally surface—if at all—much later in treatment and often only with my active encouragement. Because of both my special interest in the subject and my belief that sexual fantasies are a window into the psyche, I am more direct than most therapists in my inquiries about the subject. And yet even with me, most patients are guarded about revealing too much about what happens—or what they wish would happen—in bed.

The primary cause of this reticence is shame. Men, in particular, are ashamed of talking about what really goes on in their minds when it comes to sex. The sources of this shame are both social and psychological. In a society in which a premium is put on male sexual virility and in which homophobia is rampant, heterosexual men cannot easily admit to, much less analyze, problems with arousal, fears of women, or anything that might be seen as less than masculine. For example, men often feel ashamed about homosexual feelings, wishes for anal penetration by women, desires to be dominated, fetishes of all kinds, explicit degradation scenarios of women in which women are hurt or humiliated in some way, group sex, and sexual fantasies about very young women. There are millions of men walking around too embarrassed to admit that they have such fantasies or preferences and unable to talk frankly with their wives, girlfriends, or male friends about what arouses them and what doesn't.

Men are also more likely than women to protest that their sexual feelings have no meaning to begin with, or claim that they have no thoughts at all when they're aroused or having sex. These claims reflect more than simply a denial of the unconscious mind. Because sexual experience is located in the body, its evocation usually feels so immediate and reflexive that the notion of a complicated and meaningful story behind it can seem farfetched.

Unfortunately, such a disavowal of the deeper meanings of sexual arousal can have grim consequences. If our sexual preferences have no meaning, then there is nothing we can do with our shame and guilt other than suppress them. If our sexual fantasies and feelings have no meaning, then there is no possibility of correcting the misunderstandings about them that arise between people, no way to deepen our tolerance and empathy for each other's idiosyncratic ways of seeking pleasure.

The difficulty that we all have in divining meaning in sexual desire is precisely the reason the idea presented here that sex reflects a solution to a psychological problem can be so powerful and transformative. In response to people who tell me that they have no fantasies when they get aroused, I will often ask them if they have a preference for a partner who is tall or short, thin or heavy, or in possession of particular physical features. They invariably say yes. And when I ask them if there are some sexual positions that they enjoy more than others or sexual scenarios they've read about or seen on television or in films that they find especially arousing, they also answer in the affirmative.

I tell them that these preferences are exactly the same as sexual fantasies. Everyone has sexual preferences about what type of person turns them on, about how they like to have sex, and about the types of scenarios they find especially interesting. I explain that the meaning of these preferences is identical to that of the stories and theatrics of a traditional private fantasy. For example, the meaning behind one man's elaborate daydream about being sexually dominated by a powerful woman is probably similar to the meaning of another man's preference for tall women or another man's special excitement about being on the bottom during sex. In all three cases, the meaning is: the woman is strong enough that I don't have to feel responsible for her. In this sense, all of our sexual preferences are actually sexual fantasies. The challenge is to understand their meaning.

Both men and women also resist exploring the psychic determinants of their own sexual feelings because they have no motivation to do so. People rarely come into therapy for help understanding and changing their sexual fantasies and preferences. Men will sometimes consult with me about their sexual preferences because their wives have made upsetting discoveries of their pornography or other sexual peccadilloes or they have a sexual dysfunction of some kind. But unless pressured in some way, people generally feel little need to examine the hidden reasons for their erotic preferences. The experience of arousal and pleasure is so intrinsically positive that it eliminates one of the motives for self-exploration, namely, suffering. Even when someone suffers from sexual shame and guilt, it rarely occurs to that person that such feelings are irrational and should be more deeply understood.

Women's Resistance to Understanding Male Sexuality

While both sexes have resistances to exploring the meaning of sexuality, women will sometimes appear to make an exception when it comes to male sexual behavior. Numerous women's magazines exploit this curiosity with regular articles claiming to answer the question: what do men really want in bed? Unfortunately, women find themselves frustrated in this effort, not only because men themselves can't explain their own motivations but because of their own special blind spots. For example, many women are likely to agree with the misleading cliché that "men only want one thing" because their real experience of male sexuality seems to confirm it. Whether fending off men in a bar; feeling manipulated by men who "love 'em and leave 'em"; suffering the intrusions of sexual looking, touching, or innuendo; or being explicitly harassed in more violent ways, women regularly encounter some version of the male obsession with sex. In a context in which women often feel on the sexual defensive, they may well have difficulty looking beneath the surface of male sexual behavior and compassionately understanding the real motivations that drive it. In other words, to the extent that women feel threatened by male desire, they lack an incentive to understand its subtler determinants.

However, there are also more private and irrational sources of the tendency among many women to caricature male sexuality in this particular way. I have treated many women who avoid thinking about the complexity of men because of a covert concern that acknowledging it may weaken their own defenses and increase their vulnerability. Some women have the irrational worry that understanding male behavior means condoning it. They feel that if they view this aspect of men with more tolerance and curiosity, then they have somehow to comply with it.

Another defensive purpose served by a one-dimensional view of men is that it can help women deny conflicts about their own sexual desires. As we've seen, many women have an irrational fear of their own sexuality, and if men appear to be overly invested in sex, women can more easily suppress and deny their own investment. Women are often so guilty and ashamed about their own wishes to abandon themselves to ruthless sexual desires that they project such wishes onto men. The "problem," for the woman, then, becomes the man's sexual impulsivity and not her own. "He has only one thing on his mind" hides the fact that she has difficulty with the extent to which it's on her mind. In this way, women reproduce the cultural stereotype that "men use love to get sex" while "women use sex to get love."

Thus, for both rational and irrational reasons, women have difficulty understanding the complex logic of male desire. They cling to certain stereotypes despite being exposed to evidence that contradicts them. For example, most men who might be attracted to images of nubile femininity are also aroused by their wives. Most men don't seek out pornography as a primary sexual outlet and don't want to turn their marital bedrooms into porn stages. Most men do not cruise bars, troll for prepubescent girls in Internet chat rooms, whistle at women on the street, or hang *Penthouse* calendars in their workplaces. The point here isn't to invalidate the real experiences of male sexuality that give rise to these caricatures, but to argue that there are social and psychological resistances in women to tolerating, appreciating, and becoming curious about the actual complexity of male erotic life.

Finally, many people of both sexes are resistant to analyzing the psychology of their sexual lives because they worry that analyzing passion will dampen it or drain it of its special magic. All of us want to claim a sphere of experience that is entirely private, inaccessible to others, a place where we can imagine that we're free and outside the control and scrutiny of the public world. In this context, psychological explanations of our sexual experience can feel as if that experience is being judged and taken away from us. When it comes to the quintessentially private arena of sex, theories about its "real" dynamics are often met with a defiant insistence that this dimension of personal life is—and should be—beyond the reach of science.

The good news is that if people don't want to change their sexual preferences, psychological analysis won't affect them. The bad news is that if people do want to change their sexual preferences, analyzing them may also not change anything. It is exceedingly difficult for people to change their core sexual fantasies, their most fundamental sexual reflexes and preferences.

On the surface, this fact is puzzling. If sexual desires are the outcome of an unconscious process through which a pathogenic belief is counteracted, then it should follow that changing this underlying belief will lead to changes in a person's sexual repertoire. Consider, for example, the case of a man who has a special penchant for sexual scenarios in which he dominates women who become aroused in the process. He and I explore this fantasy and discover that the woman's arousal and willingness negates his irrational guilt and worry about hurting women. It also becomes clear that these pathogenic beliefs create problems in many other areas of his life, for example, by undermining his self-assertion in his marriage. As a result of our work on these issues, the patient's guilt and worry about women decreases and he feels more confident in his marriage. Shouldn't it follow that his sexual preferences would change as well?

Unfortunately, it doesn't usually work out that way. In my experience, our basic sexual fantasies, our default preferences about what turns us on, don't usually fundamentally change as a direct result of understanding them—in or out of therapy. That is, if someone gets especially aroused by being dominant, he or she is unlikely to become someone who becomes especially aroused by being submissive. If a man prefers sex that is a little rough because it reassures him that his partner is strong and can "take it," it's unlikely that he will be transformed into a man who gets a special thrill out of very gentle lovemaking. Understanding the psychology of our sexual desires may help us be more flexible and even more sexually experimental, but it rarely changes our core preferences.

There are two reasons that modifying our underlying pathogenic beliefs doesn't necessarily make us change our basic fantasies and preferences. First, we don't want to change our sexual fantasies. Most people want to have more sex and better sex, but not to significantly change their basic patterns of arousal. Our sexual fantasies are pleasurable. People enter therapy for help with their problems, for the suffering that their pathogenic beliefs are creating in their lives. They are highly motivated to change these beliefs in order to have more satisfaction. Sexual fantasies and preferences, however, are already satisfying. By definition, they are our preferred route to pleasure, not suffering. Therefore, people have little motivation to change their sexual desires unless they are causing someone else suffering or harm.

The second reason that there is no one-to-one correspondence between changing a pathogenic belief and changing a sexual fantasy is that while we can modify our underlying beliefs enough to lead happier lives, we rarely entirely eliminate such beliefs. Some pathogenic beliefs are universal and so hard-wired as to be only modifiable and not completely removable. For example, most people feel some residue of guilt about having more than their parents have. Children, after all, are in a different phase of the life cycle and will always have more of life ahead of them than their parents do, and this irreducible fact lays the groundwork for some form of regret or guilt. Further, children are invariably sensitive to rejection from those adults upon whom they're dependent, and such rejection is inevitable because parents cannot be completely attuned, at all times, to the needs of their children. To the extent that the shape of our sexual fantasies and preferences derives from a process in which we counteract feelings of rejection and guilt, our sexual inclinations will tend to be fairly stable.

Thus, the second reason that sexual fantasies are resistant to change is that the underlying conflicts developed in childhood are persistent, even if the bearer of these conflicts has been able to weaken their hold. In the course of healthy development—or of successful psychotherapy—pathogenic beliefs can be overcome enough to remove them as impediments to the satisfaction of major life goals, but they are not eliminated entirely. As such, they remain as vulnerabilities even as they diminish as obstacles, exerting their influence on sexual desire all the while.

So What Can People Change about Their Sexuality?

A great deal. By understanding what makes them tick in the bedroom, people can transform how they view their own sexuality and that of others and, as a result, radically enhance their pleasure, self-esteem, communication, and intimacy. By understanding that sexual responses have deeply personal and important meanings, people can develop a deeper tolerance and compassion toward themselves and their partners. They can stop blaming themselves and each other and communicate better about problems that have their origins in simple misunderstanding.

Far too many people are walking around thinking that their sexuality is abnormal and somehow "wrong." They worry that they want sex too much or little, in ways that are too "kinky" or too "uptight." Men think they're "dirty old men" for getting turned on by teenage girls or secret rapists for liking depictions of sexual domination in pornography or the mainstream media. Women worry that they aren't having enough orgasms with men or that they're hopelessly doomed to fail to live up to what they assume are the pornographic ideals of men. There are countless relationships in which the diminution of sexual interest is seen as the shameful death-knell of successful intimacy. Except for new lovers at the height of their infatuation, almost no one in our culture feels happy with their sexuality.

However, if we understood our sexuality in the right way, all of these painful judgments would decrease or disappear. When it comes to sex, there is always a method to our madness. Divining that method, the secret logic behind the sexual thoughts and actions that shame or frustrate us, can set us free of the burden of "getting it right" and open us up to the possibilities of greater pleasure with what we already have.

There are any number of ways that this can happen, in or out of therapy. By understanding that all fantasies and preferences, regardless of their intensity or content, are the outcome of a wish to feel safe, we can stop judging them according to moral criteria. People don't want good or bad sex, or sex in good or bad ways. People want to have normal pleasure and connection but have adapted honestly to their emotional upbringing and experience by developing a particular repertoire that they believe will get them this pleasure and connection. The reason that one repertoire is different from another isn't because either is healthier but because the particular fears and feelings that are being managed in each case are different, thus generating different solutions. Sexual fantasies and preferences are simply solutions to unconsciously experienced problems.

Because male sexuality so often is viewed—by both sexes—as instinctual, this shift from morality to meaning is especially important. When men are encouraged to explore the emotional sources of their sexual desires they feel less guilty about them, and this usually leads to an increase in their self-esteem. For example, my patient Ted was embarrassed about his wish to be held down and rendered helpless in bed by a woman. When he realized that he was really worried about hurting women, he felt much better.

Al, on the other hand, dealt with his worries about women by encouraging his sexual partner to "talk dirty" to him. Such sex talk, it turned out, was arousing because it reassured him that his partner loved sex and wanted it as much as he did. Al's wife, however, was somewhat offended by Al's penchant for such conversation, and Al felt guilty about liking it. Further, his wife's sensitivity led him to worry that she couldn't handle the full measure of his sexual feelings, and this led him to shut down.

When Al came to understand what he liked about talking dirty, he felt relieved and more self-accepting. When he realized that it was his wife and not he who had a problem in this instance, he was able to talk to his wife in ways that encouraged her sexual self-expression rather than threatened her.

When women are helped to understand the underlying dynamics of male sexuality, the results are almost always positive. Most important, when women learn to distinguish between men's motivation and behavior, they can begin to take the latter less personally. For example, Alice and Jon came to see me because Alice had recently discovered a large cache of pornography in a drawer in Jon's desk. She felt rejected and betrayed, and Jon responded with defensiveness and withdrawal. As we explored the situation further, it became clear that Jon was a long-suffering man who found it difficult to ask for what he needed, including in bed. The appeal of pornography lay in the fantasies they evoked of free and easy pleasure with women eager to satisfy his needs. I was able to point out to Alice that while she had every right to feel hurt and angry, Jon's use of pornography expressed his loneliness and inhibition, not his infidelity.

This formulation had the additional benefit of helping Jon overcome his defensiveness. By reducing his shame and shining a more sympathetic light on his sexual desires, the insight that pornography reflected an attempt to solve a problem rather than cause one enabled Jon to empathize with Alice and her outrage. After all, she was correct in her sense that Jon's use of pornography excluded her, not because it was primarily a sexual rejection but because it reflected Jon's real inability to open himself up to Alice. In other words, both partners were able to put themselves in each other's shoes and see the situation from the other person's point of view.

Armed with this newfound ability to empathize with each other, Jon and Alice found common ground. Jon went into therapy on his own to deal with what turned out to be lifelong feelings of loneliness. I encouraged him to speak up more about his feelings and needs with Alice, and I helped Alice respond less defensively to Jon's requests and complaints. Jon cleared out his pornography stash but didn't promise not to use it again. He did, however, learn how to better reassure Alice about his commitment to her.

This was not a miracle "cure." Jon and Alice were not blissfully happy at the end of their work with me. Understanding does not offer a panacea for sexual problems. What it does do, however, is create the conditions in which people can approach each other as complex human beings, each struggling to make sense of the world in the best way they can, motivated primarily by needs for safety, security, love, and pleasure rather than wishes to hurt or demean. It cannot be emphasized enough how important such a shift in perspective can be for people suffering from shame and guilt about their own sexuality and hurt and resentment about the sexuality of others.

Sad Moms, Distant Dads, and the Social Context of Male Sexuality

T HUS FAR, MY ANALYSIS OF SEXUALITY brackets the external world—taking it as a given—in order to more clearly focus on the private and internal meanings of sexual desire in men. And yet, in any discussion about the private meanings of sexuality, the elephant in the room is culture. The relationship of sex to masculinity can hardly be adequately understood as a personal matter between boys and their parents when our entire culture seems to invest it with such importance. Boys don't develop their sexual preferences in a vacuum—they are also socialized into them. Men don't simply objectify women only in the service of the need to be safe and reduce guilt but because everywhere they look, women are being objectified. Nubile femininity is not simply an unconscious antidepressant for men but a social icon, creating widespread ideals of beauty and merchandising opportunities for profit.

There is a huge literature describing the socialization processes through which male babies become masculine boys and boys become sexual men in our society. None of this research is necessarily incompatible with a clinical approach seeking to shine a special light on the deep interior psychological lives of men. These are parallel lines of investigation—on the one hand, studies of masculinity and male sexuality that focus on how children and adults learn social rules, the impact on boys of media, peer pressure, and the like, and, on the other hand, my project focusing on the unconscious beliefs that arise in the most intimate exchanges that boys have with their care-givers that give rise to symbolic solutions in the form of sexual fantasies. Both levels of explanation are important; neither necessarily discounts the role of the other in explaining male sexuality.

I believe, however, that there is a third type of approach that might shed additional light on how culture interacts with psychology in the cre-ation of male sexuality. Throughout our exploration of the familial origins of sexual fantasies and desire, we have repeatedly encountered depictions of unhappy mothers and emotionally absent or unreliable fathers. This is the cauldron within which the sexuality of so many of my male patients seems to have been formed. In my view, this configuration is common enough to suggest that there are larger social forces at work creating these particular family conditions, conditions in which boys routinely develop special unconscious conflicts that later generate special sexual solutions that they experience as entirely private. Male sexuality may indeed be formed as a personal response to parental psychology, but this psychology has been shaped by broader social and cultural factors.

The problem of blaming the parents—particularly the mother—arises at this point. Given the frequency with which we seem to encounter un-happy mothers in the backgrounds of the men described here, aren't we re-peating the historic tendency of psychological "experts" to hold mothers responsible for every aspect of a child's emotional life and difficulties? Women have been told that they should stay home to raise children, and then we have blamed them for being suffocating. They've been told to re-alize their potential and have careers, and then we have accused them of creating latch-key children. The negative effects on children of paternal ab-sence and abuse have, over time, also crept into explanations of childhood trauma, but such explanations still smack of the exaggerated need that many experts have to blame parents for everything that goes wrong in childhood. Aren't we doing the same thing here?

We have to differentiate between causation and blame. Parents are re-sponsible for defining their children's earliest sense of reality and beliefs about who they are supposed to be. But parents are also social beings, who are, at every moment, influenced by their relationships, work, culture, eco-nomics, and politics. And they were themselves children at one time, shaped by their own parents. When we look at the childhoods of men and find so many unhappy mothers and distant or critical fathers, we could just as easily locate the problem in a social world that seems so often to make mothers unhappy and to alienate fathers from their families.

The parents of the men who became my patients lived in a social world that had highly restrictive sex and gender roles, including those that made women the primary emotional caretakers of children, even if they worked at a job every bit as demanding as that of their husbands. And despite the unprecedented prevalence of single-parent and two-wage families today, some things have remained the same. One is that women mother. And they usually do so without the help of kinship networks or communities to support them, communities that could potentially dilute the impact of a solitary mother's psychology on her children.

The pattern of women mothering in families that are small and isolated was especially dominant among the parents of the baby boom generation. The story of this generation is a powerful example of how social history is always silently working behind the scenes of personal life. The period of ten to fifteen years following World War II was one in which fathers were expected to work and mothers to take care of children in ever-shrinking nuclear families. The statistically average American family in the 1950s was as small as it has ever been in history. The white, middle-class ideal consisted of a working father earning a "family wage" that was large enough to support a family, over which the mother ruled in her full-time job as housewife.

The demographics of the family have changed radically since the 1950s. Declining birth rates, increasing divorce rates, and the entry of mothers into the workforce in huge numbers have changed the shape of family life in America. And yet certain things are still constants. Whether or not they also work outside the home, women are still the primary emotional caretakers of children. And fathers are, if anything, more absent physically and at least as absent emotionally as they were in the 1950s. Whether we're speaking of parents in 1950 or 2007, the social fact remains that women are primarily responsible for caring for children, and they do so in relative isolation. Decades of feminist research has shown the deleterious effects of these social arrangements on the psychology of women who mother, the various forms of self-blaming, anxiety, guilt, and loneliness that isolated nuclear families generate in their female guardians. To the extent that this experience affects how these mothers behave and what feelings they communicate to their children, it is obvious that social life has a powerful effect on the development of children.

Fathers are crucial as well, but in a different way and usually at a different point in time. Fathers today may be important in their absence.

Nearly 30 percent of children in the United States currently live in single-parent families, almost all of which are headed by mothers. The physical absence of a father from the home not only directly affects children, but also has significant implications for the economic health of the family—a factor that contributes to the emotional stresses and strains of the mother. In addition, even in intact families with two working parents, it is the mother who is the primary object of attachment for, and spends the most time with, the child. This is particularly true in early childhood, which is so important for later psychological health. And these mothers have experienced all the pressures and strains that flow from a world in which power is unevenly distributed between the sexes and in which women often feel disadvantaged. Such experience is damaging to their emotional health and is reflected, in part, in the many ways that they're unhappy, feel cheated, or are unfulfilled. Shouldn't we, then, expect that children would be affected by this damage?

Thus, the answer here isn't to blame mothers. The problem lies in the way society treats men and women and raises children, not in the theory that describes the outcomes of this treatment. In short, the nuclear family in which a child grows up is part of a much larger society. And the stresses of that society directly affect the child through their impact on the psychological state of the parents.

An example of this lies close to home. My mother was the youngest of five girls, raised in a working-class community in northern New Jersey by a mother who was widowed when my mother was about eight years old. My grandmother was someone who, by all accounts, seemed to take it as a personal betrayal that her husband had died so young and left her with the responsibility of raising a large family. She was a martyr and barely concealed her resentment of men. Whenever one of her daughters had trouble with a man—and many of them did—she would tell them "I told you so. He was always a son of a bitch. You can't trust men." But my mother was a highly social and popular girl growing up, a cheerleader, and she enjoyed the freedom that working gave her. She worked in various offices in town, including as a teller in the local bank. She was considered beautiful and was actively pursued by many boys throughout high school.

She met my father, a boy from her hometown, just as World War II was ending. According to my mother, my father was different from other boys. He came from an uneducated family but was brilliant and highly motivated to go to college; he was also a political liberal in a conservative community. My mother later told me that not only did she admire my father in his own right, but she was taken with how he was different from anyone she knew, that he was cut from some exciting new cloth. My father seemed to offer the promise of a life, intellectual and otherwise, that was far beyond what she had ever expected or hoped for.

My father was the youngest son in a family of German descent headed by a charismatic but bullying father and a very passive and martyred mother. He was drawn to my mother because she was sexy, energetic, and always upbeat—qualities that stood in stark contrast to the chronically depressed moods of his own mother. In other words, my father experienced my mother's buoyancy and cheerful sexuality as a potential antidote to the repressive environment of his childhood. In the midst of postwar American exuberance and opportunity, my parents entered adult life full of promise and possibility.

My father was good at math and engineering, but these were not his passion. Instead, my father wanted to be a radio announcer or an actor. He had a beautiful speaking voice, was enamored of the medium of radio, and had a gift for theatricality that he had secretly always wanted to develop. But it was 1946, and he had little money, a new wife, and a baby on the way. He decided that he had to pursue economic security over personal ambition and went to Yale, where he majored in mathematics and engineering, graduated with honors, and quickly landed a job with Bell Telephone Laboratories, the research arm of AT&T. He began commuting to Manhattan every day on the train with thousands of other men.

My father didn't hate his job. He liked engineering and was a talented enough manager to rise through the corporate ranks. But he didn't pursue his deepest aspirations. Few men did in those days. Instead, they gave up their private dreams in exchange for the American Dream. Men were breadwinners, wives were raising children, and people were moving away from the ethnic neighborhoods and extended families in which they had been raised. They were moving to suburbs that sprang up everywhere promising upward mobility, but also creating longer commutes and an increased isolation of family life. Our family knew no one in the suburban township to which we moved. The houses and yards were bigger and much farther apart than the row houses of my parents' youth, architecturally symbolizing our liberation from the constraints of family and community life. When we would visit extended family in my parents' old neighborhood, one of us would say, "Look how close all the houses are to each other," an obligatory and disdainful comment that reassured us that we were better off in our spacious tract home than enmeshed in the oppressive communities from which we'd sprung. Never mind that this move was the beginning of my family's slow deterioration into depression and alcoholism—we were "making it" in America.

My parents experienced a crucial moment early on in their relationship that captured many of the gender contradictions of their time. My mother was working in a bank when she and my father first met and eventually decided to marry. The week before their wedding my mother told my father that she was quitting her job because it was now his job to support her, and that her mother had told her that "women didn't work" if they didn't absolutely have to. This was, in fact, true. The concept of the "family wage" in the 1950s meant that the man would be paid enough to support the entire family without anyone else having to work. Years later my mother told me that in fact she had liked working but felt that she was supposed to be a mother and housewife and be taken care of. It was a role that her mother and sisters had always aspired to, and she couldn't imagine making a different choice. My father remembers accepting this pronouncement calmly and agreeably because that was also his sense of how women were supposed to be. He also remembers feeling a sharp sense of disappointment and resentment. He had liked the fact that my mother seemed so independent and buoyant, and, on a level that was barely conscious, he felt the weight on his shoulders begin to grow. Neither of them could possibly have discussed this or seriously entertained another path, but it is striking that in retrospect they both felt that this new marital contract represented a loss as well as a gain.

My mother gave up her independence and my father gave up the promise of pursuing a personal ambition. Neither knew what they were giving up, nor could either have realistically violated the rules and expectations of their families and their culture. Each one was repeating the past but also complying with their broader social roles. And yet each suffered as a result, and that suffering fermented and grew over the years in ways that affected their children and eventually led to the dissolution of their relationship. My father turned to alcohol and began to withdraw from my mother and his children. He often appeared burdened by the responsibilities of his life and rarely experienced much joy. My mother became increasingly unhappy and began behaving as an unappreciated martyr, much as her own mother had done.

It was in this context that I developed my beliefs, both pathogenic and not, about what women and men were really all about, what one could expect from women and how masculinity should be defined. I learned that women were, at heart, fundamentally unhappy with their lot and that it was the man's responsibility to make them happy. Men were not only responsible but stoic. They didn't reveal their needs because it was shameful and selfish to do so. And ultimately I learned that men were alone.

This is a story that I see repeated over and over among the male patients I treat. Despite the enormous individual variation in childhood experiences, I frequently hear stories about mothers who were often withdrawn, worried, unfulfilled in their vocations and avocations, and unhappy in their marriages. And I frequently hear about relationships with fathers that were unrequited, distant, or else were combative and critical. I am not suggesting that these types of family configurations are universal, but that they are common enough to warrant our attention. And given that such childhood experiences play an important role in the ways that boys grow up and the psychological inhibitions and anxieties that they feel—all of which influence the shape of their later sexual behavior—this type of historical narrative is a vital part of understanding male sexuality.

As my story suggests, there are many ways in which the world affects the psyche, the most important of which is through the psyches of one's parents. These social contexts are the environments within which sexual desires and inhibitions are shaped. There are also factors rooted more deeply in the process of emotional development. As I described in an earlier chapter, a great deal of research has been done that demonstrates that boys, in order to both separate from their mothers and establish a masculine identity, must deny their identifications with their mothers and devalue the feelings and vulnerability that they associate with their mothers. Masculinity in our culture has a negative implication—it is not feminine. The boy's normal and healthy move toward autonomy is burdened with the job of differentiating not only from the person of his mother but from her gender as well. Femininity becomes associated with the soft and intimate world of feelings and relationships, and thus the boy devalues and flees from this realm at the same time that he is trying to establish his own separate place in the world. His developmental push away from home tends to be more forceful, and his vigilance against being a "mama's boy" has to become quite strict.

The boy's boundaries therefore tend to become more rigid, and he comes to view his own needs—which didn't disappear just because they were suppressed—as threats to his autonomy and gender role. His wishes to be close to his mother—and later to other people—are increasingly discouraged and repressed. The result is a personality that is well adapted to conditions of emotional isolation and deprivation but poorly adapted to the world of love and intimacy. Men are like camels, adapted over thousands of years to surviving in the absence of water. Camels did so by developing biological systems that are extremely efficient in using and reusing small amounts of water. Similarly, men have adapted to the relatively deprived conditions of their own childhoods by developing the ability to go for long periods with very little emotional nourishment. Unlike camels, however, they pay a price, and the price is a painful sense of disconnectedness.

When a boy cuts himself off from his mother and the interdependency that marked that early relationship, it doesn't mean he stops loving his mother or truly detaches from her. Over and over again I see men whose relationships with their mothers have been highly ambivalent and full of conflict. They still long for closeness, for caretaking, and for a relationship safe enough to tolerate dependency. In other words, their attachment needs vie with their separation needs. The result is often a sense of being trapped and an urgent need to disconnect completely. After all, sometimes these sons were their mothers' confidantes, other times the vehicle for their mothers' own secret ambitions. Sometimes they felt that they were supposed to make up for something missing in their mothers' lives or in their mothers' relationships with their fathers. And still other times these men felt that they had to watch on the sidelines while their mothers struggled with depression and frustration, as well as with the hardships that life presented to women responsible for families on the economic or social margins. These relationships were supposed to be severed as the sons grew up to be men and adopted the mantle of independence and masculinity, all the while still burdened with feelings of worry, guilt, and responsibility about their mothers' well-being.

The private and social dimensions of male development are constantly interacting. Because of the social fact that women are the primary caretakers in early childhood, and that they often perform this role in relative isolation, the mother-child relationship is especially burdened with importance. That is, boys' anxieties about identifying too much with or being too dependent on their mothers are exaggerated because Mom is the only emotional game in town. The importance of the child's emotional attachment to his mother is amplified by the social fact that attachment opportunities are limited in nuclear families. Thus, the opportunities that are there—particularly the one with the mother—assume an inordinate importance.

This quandary around attachment and autonomy defines the lives of many men in our society. They're supposed to take care of women, and yet it's dangerous to get too close to them. They imagine that they are supposed to protect, rescue, and satisfy women and yet not expect too much in return, because needing too much from women makes men vulnerable to losing their sense of difference and to identifying with someone of a gender that they've spent their lives trying not to be like. In our culture, men are almost automatically inclined to feel burdened and disconnected in their emotional lives.

Male Sexuality as a Flight from Responsibility and Guilt

As my male patients were growing up attempting to individuate from mothers burdened by their social roles—a burden that Betty Friedan called "the problem with no name"—they were also responding to fathers beset by their own social dilemmas. In her book *The Hearts of Men*, Barbara Ehrenreich argues that the traditional male breadwinner role in post–World War II America was full of contradictions. Men who weren't married were seen as less than masculine, while married men were increasingly viewed by sociologists, media pundits, and perhaps by many of the men themselves as unfairly burdened by the excessive consumption patterns of their wives and the alienation of their work roles in the burgeoning new corporate bureaucracies. One response to these burdens was the emergence of a new masculine ideal epitomized in Hugh Hefner's "Playboy philosophy." Men, Hefner said, were being domesticated by wives who were spending all their husbands' hard-earned money and restricting their freedom and sexuality. The Playboy bunny was presented as the ideal woman—sexual, eager to please, and demanding nothing in return. At the same time, men were encouraged to be more selfish and indulge themselves by buying more consumer goods.

Hefner offered men a fantasy in which they could be free of emotional commitments without having their masculinity questioned. In fact, monogamy and sexual fidelity were considered less masculine than the free sexuality of the swinging bachelor. The combination of sexual pleasure without strings attached and the increased advertising-driven consumption of material goods functioned as a balm for the hidden psychic damage that men allegedly endured at the hands of parasitic wives and work environments that seemed to demand conformity and even a spiritual estrangement. Faced with a choice in the 1950s between two narratives of masculinity—"Hef" in a bathrobe (a symbol of sexual leisure), surrounded by bunnies in the "mansion," and Dagwood Bumstead henpecked by his wife, Blondie, and dominated by his boss—it is no wonder that men began to rebel against marital commitment and responsibility.

Of course, in the real world one usually can't choose to live in a narrative. Real men, as opposed to fantasy men, have needs for security, commitment, family, paternity, and community, none of which is ultimately compatible with the Playboy philosophy. But the powerful appeal of this ideal suggests that in postwar America, men lived lives that felt burdened and isolated enough that the Playboy lifestyle could be popularized as an escape or solution.

These contradictions in the male psyche and social role were played out over and over again between men and their wives and children. Work became a refuge from the demands of family life and yet didn't itself often offer deep satisfactions. Increasing time away from home meant increasing paternal absence, and sons and daughters suffered as a result. Among other things, paternal absence meant that increasing numbers of boys and girls were growing up neither knowing what their fathers did, nor what masculinity and fatherhood were really all about.

At every moment, social pressures as well as highly personal ones were shaping these fathers and their families. My own father, for example, was caught up in the postwar definitions of "the good life," as well as simultaneously repeating his childhood relationships with his parents. Men of my father's generation internalized the definitions of success being promoted in the culture at that time, ideals that featured upward financial mobility, almost limitless access to consumer goods, and a house and family in the suburbs. At the same time, my father and his peers were also working out their own personal relationships with their families of origin. The interaction between these cultural ideals and private conflicts defined many of their choices.

External and internal forces are always in play. The Playboy message that men were being coerced into sacrificing personal pleasures on the altar of marital and familial responsibility could just as well have been directed at my father's childhood feelings of guilt and responsibility for taking care of his depressed and unhappy mother. My mother's hopeful wish to be taken care of, as well as her disappointment and martyred depression when she wasn't—both inevitable outgrowths of the postwar feminine role—repeated both her and her mother's childhood relationships with their fathers. Both parents, and all adults, are simultaneously social and individual actors.

In her analysis of the plight of contemporary American men, *Stiffed*, Susan Faludi gives an even more nuanced account of the experience of paternal absence and its effects on boys following World War II. She tells story after story of fathers who were emotionally absent and therefore couldn't help their sons grow up knowing how to be. Her interviews with men convey an undercurrent of their longing for male guidance, some tradition to step into, some sense of belonging that they imagined they would find once they reached adulthood. Instead, Faludi hears stories of fathers who left home after divorces or withdrew emotionally when they were home, or were bullies who frightened everyone in their families.

Faludi argues that the men of my father's generation who returned from a war in which values like loyalty, teamwork, and "getting the job done" were publicly embraced, gradually felt betrayed in their work and communities. Workplaces were increasingly automated, and the image of the bureaucrat or drone began to define many work roles. Corporations in the 1960s and 1970s began to lay off workers and move operations overseas. Sports teams picked up and left town without any regard for fan loyalty. And images of male celebrity—the sports or Hollywood star, the Marlboro Man and other icons of advertising—became the ideal of masculinity, replacing the older ideals of the craftsman, community elder, or the entrepreneur who could pass along wisdom to the next generation.

In such a context, boys growing up in the 1950s and 1960s felt fatherless, rudderless in their efforts to define who and what men were supposed to be. Faludi is describing another dimension of the special alienation and disconnectedness that plague men, the breakdown of social bonds of loyalty, community, and male camaraderie and mentorship that could otherwise counteract the undertow of guilt and loneliness that tended to be generated in a boy's psychological development.

The sexual remedies that people use as antidotes to pathogenic beliefs formed in relationships with unhappy mothers and absent or unhappy fathers are fully comprehensible only if understood in their social context. The social context and an individual's private experience are two different levels of explanation for the same phenomena. I have presented one "story" of how these different dimensions intersected in the intimate exchanges in families that were, themselves, burdened by the social and cultural expectations of post–World War II America. There are other stories to be told in today's society, of course. The point is that the personal and political, the social and psychological, are always interacting in complicated ways that are usually opaque to us as individuals. My baby boom patients did not understand, of course, that their mothers were miserable because of the dissatisfaction that so many women in the 1950s felt about suburban domesticity.

They didn't know or care that their fathers' alienation and malaise was being described in social terms by William Whyte in *The Organization Man* and David Riesman in *The Lonely Crowd*. Nor do children today have the objectivity to appreciate the degree to which their stressed-out mothers go off to their paid jobs in the morning feeling racked with guilt for leaving their children and resentful of the uneven division of household labor that exists in even the most enlightened homes today. Children are attached to and dependent on Mom or Dad and develop their beliefs, pathogenic and otherwise, in the course of interacting with these unique individuals. Children relate only to individuals, but understanding the origins of these private relationships must involve understanding their public dimension. Only then can one compassionately understand the true meaning of the sexual solutions that each gender creatively generates to solve what ails them.

The Politics of
Male Sexuality

WHEN IT COMES TO SEXUALITY, politics can cloud our judgment, impair our compassion, restrict our tolerance, and threaten our capacity for critical thinking. Our history is replete with examples of how political agendas have influenced scientific inquiry, from the Scopes monkey trial and its descendants today in the creationist movement, to the current restrictions on stem-cell research. The field of sexuality is especially prone to political exploitation because it is so closely connected with issues of censorship and freedom of speech, women's rights, homosexuality, the sanctity of marriage and the family, and the power struggles between adults and children—all arenas that have provoked bitter political struggles.

Increasingly, the battleground has shifted from what people do sexually to what they think. A young Ohio man named Brian Dalton, having served time in prison on child pornography charges, was paroled in 1998 and lived with his mother while on probation. One morning, Dalton's mother found his private journal, which contained descriptions of the rape and torture of three young girls. Hoping to get her son further help, she turned the diary over to his probation officer who passed it along to the District Attorney. Dalton was charged with "pandering obscenity involving a minor" and entered into a plea bargain that netted him seven years in prison. The fact that Dalton never intended his diary to be made public, as well as the fact that the accounts in it were entirely fictional, didn't dissuade the prosecutor from viewing him as a danger to society. It's hard to avoid the conclusion that Brian Dalton ended up in prison for his thoughts.

The move from prohibiting actions to outlawing thoughts has gained momentum with the advent of the Internet and the wide availability of sexual content online to people of all ages. The Supreme Court recently upheld the constitutionality of a law passed by Congress, which outlawed, among other things, "any virtual depiction that appears to be promoted to convey the impression that the material is of a minor engaging in sexually explicit conduct." Historically, child pornography was considered obscene and illegal because real children were used and abused in its production. Congress took the radical position that the mere representation of a child in a sexual situation should be outlawed, even if that representation did not involve a real child—for example, if it were entirely computer generated. Since it could not be empirically shown that consuming either real or virtual child pornography increased the likelihood of real pedophilia, the only explanation for this provision was that Congress believed that thinking bad thoughts should be outlawed.

There are great dangers in collapsing the distinctions between sexual thoughts and deeds, fantasy and reality, and private and public. Fantasies don't usually lead to action. Fantasies are often compensatory, providing us comfort when reality can't. Fantasies also often depict scenarios that are the opposite of what we really want or do. As I have shown, a man who wants to be able to be strong without worrying about hurting women might fantasize about hurting a woman who becomes progressively aroused in the process. The manifest fantasy is abusive; the underlying motivation is not. Unfortunately, legislators tend to judge the book by its cover and take the overt content of a fantasy or thought as the "real" meaning. Psychological depth is eliminated, and with it goes much of the imaginative life of the human unconscious mind.

The current politicization of sex by conservative politicians and pundits risks exaggerating the sexual guilt and shame that most of us already feel. Sexual desire is seen by ideologues as something that, in principle, has to be contained and controlled, a view that can reinforce our own internal prohibitions and conflicts about these same desires. As both the Brian Dalton case and recent antipornography legislation illustrate, there is a new wave of sexual censorship and prohibition that, like puritanical movements of the past, views thoughts and feelings as identical to actions in the danger they pose to a proper moral society. When schools are told that they have to teach children that the only good form of birth control is abstinence, they are in fact telling children that their own natural sexual desires are bad and dangerous. The subtext of much conservative rhetoric is that people should feel guilty and ashamed of their sexual feelings. And the more that our sexuality is suppressed, the more we seek out forbidden forms of it.

The stakes are high. Our ability to understand and tolerate the existence of a private psychological world insulated from social regulation is gradually declining. As sex becomes more and more of a political battleground, and the distinctions between fantasy and reality, private and public, and conscious and unconscious begin breaking down, sexuality comes to be viewed as a dangerous time bomb, just waiting to explode. The logic is: "If men are aroused by erotic depictions of teenage girls, they must want to have sex with them. And if they want to have sex with them, they're likely to go out and do it." Some people today assume that if teenagers know the facts about pregnancy, masturbation, and sexually transmitted diseases, that knowledge will then lead to more sexual behavior. If abortion is legal, then women will supposedly use it as a form of birth control and become more promiscuous. And if teenagers or adults have access to sexual material on the Internet, they will be more likely to act out in inappropriate or dangerous ways. Girls will be seduced by Internet predators and boys and men will become emboldened to act out what they see on their computer monitors. There is no hard evidence supporting any of these fears, and yet a wave of panic is being stirred up in which we are increasingly being held responsible for our thoughts, fantasies, and dreams as if they were facts of the social world rather than dramas in the private world of our imaginations.

When distinctions between thought and action or fantasy and reality begin to break down, the societal debate about sexuality is forced into rigidly held black-and-white categories, full of posturing about good and evil. In such an atmosphere, pointing out the complexity of sexual desire is urgently needed, even as the space for such discussions is collapsing around us. Believing in the unconscious mind, much less the highly developed theory of sexual arousal presented here, becomes radical in the current political environment.

Innocence and the Demonization of Pedophilia

Thus, we are frequently tempted to respond to the surface meaning of sexuality rather than explore it in depth, particularly when it comes to male sexuality. And, as chapter 5 illustrated, nowhere is this more true than when it comes to pedophilia. The key question, however, is still "Why?" Why do we hold the pedophile up as the worst, the most evil of all criminals?

There is clearly an imbalance in our collective scales of crime and punishment. The California judge who heard the case of accused child molester Jerome Wilhoit told his courtroom during Wilhoit's arraignment that if someone had molested his own daughter, his attitude would be "you touch her, you die." The trial was on the front page. The fact that Wilhoit was not only acquitted on all charges but was later deemed to be "factually innocent"—an unusual legal ruling—didn't quite make it to page one. Another example is the infamous case from the 1980s involving the McMartin preschool, a case lasting six years, costing the State of California $15 million, in which over 400 children were interviewed by so-called experts. The defendants were acquitted on all counts.

I realize that for every instance of a false accusation based on false memory there are dozens of cases of unreported abuse, and that the advent in the 1970s and 1980s of laws regarding the reporting of child abuse brought important victories for child protection advocates. Nevertheless, I think that our collective outrage at sexual abuse so dwarfs our recognition of other forms of childhood trauma that it behooves us to ask why.

The reason that sexual abuse occupies such a privileged place in the pantheon of bad things done to children cannot be that such abuse causes the greatest harm. If you ask most psychotherapists to describe the most devastating traumas they see in the lives of the children they treat or in the childhoods of their adult patients, sexual molestation usually would not be at the top of their lists. In statistics released by the Department of Health and Human Services in 2002, over 60 percent of the officially reported cases of maltreatment of children involved neglect, while barely 10 percent involved sexual abuse. In my own practice, I see the damage done by neglect and other forms of emotional deprivation much more than I do the trauma of sexual abuse.

It may seem callous to attempt to rank traumas, especially since there is no doubt that sexual abuse is extremely harmful to its childhood victims. But the high prevalence of neglect and emotional deprivation highlights the puzzling fact that these conditions may not only corrupt childhood innocence more and leave deeper psychological scars than pedophilia, but they are also more insidious because they are relatively invisible. Neglect—referring not only to the absence of the parent but also to particular disturbances in the relationship to a parent—is one example. By virtue of either psychological or social pathology, many parents are unable to provide a secure and protective connection to their children, systematically ignore their children's emotional cues, resort to violence or shaming as forms of discipline, or use their children to mirror and remedy their own attachment needs. This results in a situation every bit as neglectful of the child's needs as one in which the parents are simply absent. Such children grow up with terribly low self-esteem, lack the ability to comfort themselves, and feel guilty and responsible for their own suffering. They have a hard time feeling empathy for others, including their own children, and can't create and sustain a loving relationship. They feel disconnected and undeserving of the good things in life, develop depressions and severe anxiety disorders, and may often turn to drugs or violence in order to numb these feelings. These handicaps usually last a lifetime and are often passed on to the next generation. The human devastation is profound.

Further, social and economic hardship in a culture that celebrates financial success surely worsens the harm done to children by unhealthy attachments. While emotional neglect and abuse spans all social classes, the strains of economic insecurity, poverty, and racism, along with the absence of social support and services—including those aimed directly at children—for poor and working families inevitably leave children especially unprotected and psychologically vulnerable. Twenty-seven million children—37 percent of all children in America today—are categorized by the Census Bureau as "near-poor" or poor, defined here as a family of three earning $27,000 or less per year. Nine million children are without any health insurance. Many of these children are being psychologically damaged each and every day by an environment that seems at times to not see them, hear them, or take care of them.

I'm not equating the psychological harm of poverty and illness to that of sexual abuse, but I am pointing out that when pathological caretaking interacts with a social environment filled with hardship, the psychological damage that befalls such children is accentuated. And yet the children imperiled by neglect, indifference, and poverty don't appear on milk cartons; they aren't plastered on the front pages of our newspapers and don't appear as the lead story on CNN. Typically, no one goes to jail for the crime of "narcissistically using her child as an extension of herself," or "demeaning his children because he feels demeaned," or "being so drunk and depressed that his children have to raise themselves." And yet, punishment is supposed to fit the crime, and the crime consists of the amount of damage done to the victim. Perhaps, then, the punishment we mete out to sexual abusers is a function of factors other than the harm they do to children.

The demonization of the sexual abuser has become so strong that raising these questions in public has itself become dangerous, eliciting a similar type of outrage and condemnation as the act of sexual abuse itself, and no doubt for the same reasons. There are many examples of political attacks on intellectuals who have dared to challenge or raise questions about the logic or politics underlying our extreme hatred of the pedophile. Judith Levine's incisive analysis of the conservative political agendas behind current trends in sex education, abortion, and censorship, *Harmful to Minors: The Perils of Protecting Children from Sex*, came under attack before it was even published. Various conservative groups tried to have it withdrawn or censored. Robert Knight, director of Concerned Women for America's Culture and Family Institute in Washington, D.C., condemned it as "very evil." Tim Pawlenty, then majority leader of the Minnesota House of Representatives, labeled it "trash" and demanded that the University of Minnesota cease publication. Nationally syndicated conservative talk shows including *The Dr. Laura Schlessinger Program* and Michael Savage's *Savage Nation* railed against it, despite the admission by Dr. Laura that she had only skimmed the book. And the editorial board of the *Lancaster New Era* in Pennsylvania declared, "This is a sick book and the University of Minnesota is sick for publishing it."

An even more egregious attempt to squelch serious scientific thought and debate about the issue of child sexual abuse was reflected in the firestorm of controversy over the work of Bruce Rind and his collaborators at Temple University. In 1998, Rind et al. published a paper entitled "A Meta-Analytic Examination of Assumed Properties of Child Sexual Abuse Using College Samples" in a prestigious and refereed journal published by the American Psychological Association (APA). The authors analyzed fifty-nine studies of college freshmen who had been sexually abused as children, and, using widely accepted statistical techniques, evaluated the correlations reported in these studies between the subjects' sexual abuse and their later psychological development. Rind and his coauthors found that, contrary to popular opinion, it was impossible to definitively conclude that sexual abuse always caused severe and lasting psychological damage.

The Rind study instead found that the psychological impact of sexual abuse was greatly influenced by other factors, including the victims' family environment, age, and gender. Although the overall psychological adjustment of the subjects who experienced sexual abuse was slightly lower than those who did not, there were obvious differences among the victims, for example, between a girl raped by her father at age six and a fourteen-year-old boy having oral sex with an older unrelated man. In fact, the research showed that girls were more traumatized by sexual contact with adults than were boys. In some of the studies that Rind reviewed, a significant number of boys reported that they even found the experience to be a positive one. Rind's article concluded that the validity of most studies of nonclinical populations that correlate sexual abuse with mental illness in adults are flawed, primarily because their methodological problems lead them to overestimate these correlations. They go on to argue that this doesn't mean that there is no relationship, but that we need much better studies to prove it. Finally, Rind and his colleagues state that pedophilia may justly be held as morally and legally wrong, but that "harmfulness cannot be equated with wrongfulness."

Unfortunately, this distinction was lost on certain groups and individuals who launched a vituperative attack on Rind, his research, and the APA for publishing a paper that they claimed "condoned" pedophilia. Dr. Laura accused the APA of using "junk science" to endorse sex between adults and children and, in an unprecedented politicization of scientific research, in the summer of 1999, the United States House of Representatives voted 355–0 to condemn this particular study. Most of the members hadn't read Rind's study, of course, but that didn't stop the minority whip, Tom DeLay, from saying, "I am appalled and outraged that an influential American psychological association would publish a study that advocates normalizing pedophilia." Of course, serious researchers also challenged Rind's findings. My point isn't that Rind was right or wrong but that temperate scientific debate was impossible.

Obviously, child sexual abuse has meanings that ignite our passions and trigger our desire for vengeance. In my clinical experience, when people feel this degree of outrage about an offense that they themselves did not directly experience, that offense—and offender—invariably turn out to have a symbolic meaning that goes beyond the event itself, a meaning that stimulates conflicts and resonates with feelings about which people have no awareness. We have seen this type of extreme punitive indignation throughout history in response to classes of people by whom we feel especially threatened. Fantasies among whites, particularly in the South, about black men having sex with white women provoked enormous anxiety and retaliatory rage and led to violent racist persecutions. Our paranoid fears and persecutions of alleged Communists during the 1950s were similarly based on irrational fantasies about conspiratorial and malevolent outsiders infiltrating our God-fearing society and taking over. The image of bra-burning feminists in the 1970s who wanted to control men was a mythic creation of men threatened by the specter of female independence. And, of course, we have always demonized homosexuals because, I believe, we are frightened and guilty about our own longings for closer contact with members of our own sex. Throughout our history, we have created symbolic narratives rife with incendiary images about certain groups who psychologically threaten us, and who provoke our moral indignation and justify our defensive retaliation.

Of course, unlike blacks, Communists, feminists, and gays, pedophiles do hurt others and need to be stopped. But, like these other groups, our culture has made the pedophile larger than life, his prevalence exaggerated, and his danger overstated. He is both a real problem and an invented one. It's easy to understand the rational component of our fear of and hostility toward an adult who molests a child—after all, the power relationship is unequal, the motive is exploitive, and the trauma is genuine. But what about the irrational component of our reaction? What threatens us about the pedophile? Why is no punishment too severe for him, no restriction of his rights too unfair? Why does the act of sexually molesting a child seem to command our collective outrage and desire for vengeance while acts of ignoring, humiliating, or starving that same child do not?

Some social critics, such as James Kincaid, have suggested that we romanticize the sexual innocence of childhood in order to deny our awareness of the nuances of erotic desire that normally exist between adults and children. Since the time of Freud, the sexuality of children has been hotly debated. Most experts—and many parents—would agree that children are sexual beings, that they have the capacity for sexual pleasure even if they don't always understand how to regulate it. And there is equally no doubt that adults sometimes have sexual feelings for children. Any parent who has watched a son or daughter come of age is aware of how powerful these feelings of attraction can be and to what lengths both parties go to avoid this embarrassing tension. Certainly there can be no doubt about the sexual energy inherent in adolescence, since it is constantly exploited by advertisers who use images of nubile girls and boys to sell everything from jeans to soft drinks.

Yet it is equally true that our consciences are especially intolerant of incestuous forms of sexuality. The incest taboo is universal; human beings work hard to repress their awareness of any semblance of erotic feeling toward children. Therefore, theorists like Kincaid argue, the scene is set for us to externalize the conflict and direct our punitive judgments at the pedophile rather than our own impulses. We defensively desexualize ourselves and our children in order to reassure ourselves and others that we are free of any sexual desires even remotely connected to childhood.

The appeal of this theory derives from its intuitive grasp of the passionate ambivalence with which we approach childhood sexuality and its abuse. We are horrified by the kidnap/murder of JonBenét Ramsey, but can't get enough videotape footage of her displays of adult sexuality at junior beauty pageants. High schools try to enforce dress codes, while their students are inundated by erotic advertising messages. Brooke Shields's depiction of a twelve-year-old prostitute in Louis Malle's film *Pretty Baby* was considered risqué and banned by the Catholic Church, but the ensuing controversy helped ticket sales. Perhaps, as Kincaid suggests, we censor and attack those desires in others that we find unacceptable in ourselves.

There are, however, other deep-seated desires that are at least as forbidden and repressed as incestuous ones, longings that people in our culture cannot tolerate in themselves and, as a result, need to project onto the childhood victims of sexual abuse. I am referring to feelings of helplessness and innocence. People in our society cannot compassionately face their own innocent victimization—an experience suffered in several different contexts—and, instead, project it onto the images they create of the virginal, sexually virtuous, and naive child. I would argue that one of the reasons that our defense of childhood virtue and innocence is so extreme is because it bundles with it all of the ways that we, ourselves, feel—but cannot acknowledge feeling—unfairly taken advantage of, betrayed, subordinated to the self-interests of others, and helpless.

The notion that we are resistant to feeling helpless and innocent is by no means obvious. After all, don't we live in, as one author put it, a "culture of complaint"? Aren't we becoming a therapy culture in which everything is blamed on our parents? Weren't the 1960s and 1970s, in fact, marked by people eschewing personal responsibility, expecting the government to take care of them, and blaming the dominant culture for every injury, slight, or disadvantage that befell them? From this perspective, claims of innocence and helplessness seem more like a growing social problem than a forbidden truth.

However, what some social critics don't understand is that there is a correlation between how loudly someone proclaims his or her innocence and victimization, and how responsible and guilty that person actually feels inside. Most people can't tolerate feeling guilty and self-blaming for long. They either internalize or externalize it. If they internalize it, they get depressed. If they externalize it, they attempt to convince themselves and others that they're innocent victims and act martyred and blaming. The unconscious message, then, is: "I'm not guilty, I'm innocent; I haven't victimized anyone or done anything wrong, I'm actually a helpless victim. It's your fault, not mine." Claims of innocence often reflect efforts to deny the opposite. A modern compulsion to hold others responsible—whether it's parents, the "system," or the government—rather than ourselves is actually a testament to how guilty we really feel, not how innocent.

Attempts to counteract feelings of guilt by declaring our innocence and lack of responsibility, however, don't work for long. Our internal critics may be quieted but are never eliminated, because the real sources of our guilt are irrational and continually reinforced. As a result, we have to continually project blame outward whenever we can in order to relieve this internal pressure.

In my clinical experience, the only way for people to take realistic responsibility for their lives is to stop feeling unrealistically responsible. They have to feel less responsible for things that aren't their fault in order to feel more responsible for things that are under their control. Similarly, the only way for people to feel true innocence is to face the ways that they feel irrationally guilty, and to locate responsibility for their troubles where it actually belongs.

How do people figure out where blame actually does belong? What is the difference between rational and irrational responsibility and guilt? The answer requires that we understand why these questions are difficult to begin with. And that difficulty begins in childhood. Children have an innate tendency to take responsibility for everything around them, even though they are, in fact, less responsible for their relationships and environments than they will ever be in their lives. Parents have enormous power to define who children come to feel they are and who they're supposed to be. The parent-child relationship is a two-way street, to be sure, but the traffic is much heavier going from parent to child than vice versa. The relationship is mutual but asymmetrical.

My clinical experience has taught me, however, that when bad things happen, children irrationally, but secretly, feel that it's their fault. It's their fault if their parents divorce, are angry, or get depressed. Children are constantly monitoring their parents' moods and trying to make sense of them. If a parent becomes unhappy, a child will not only tend to feel responsible for causing the unhappiness, but responsible for fixing it. And if the parent's unhappiness is, in fact, actually directed at the child, the child's guilt becomes even worse, because children almost always comply with their parents' view of them. If they're rejected, they comply and feel undeserving. If they're abandoned, they come to believe that they're difficult to love. If their parents are weak and needy, the children automatically come to feel responsible for their caretakers and guilty about their own legitimate interests. Children resist—and continue to resist, as adults—acknowledging their own innocence.

It is said that people would, by and large, prefer to be "sinners in heaven than saints in hell" in the sense that they would prefer to believe that they have a just and good family in which they were bad than a bad family in which they were good. For this reason, abused children often report that they provoked their parents' violence, and adults often qualify accounts of their own early beatings with the caveat that they were "difficult" children. Most people can't let themselves feel innocent, because in a truly moral universe their caregivers would then have to be guilty, and that recognition is intolerable. It would mean that they, as children, were not protected; that the attachment necessary to their psychological survival was absent, disturbed, or even dangerous; and that the beings upon whom they helplessly depended might, at times, have meant harm. Children can rarely face this emotional reality, and neither can most adults. It is not even necessary that these perceptions be objectively true—it is the subjective experience of parental failures that is so frightening that it leads to self-blaming.

At the end of the first season of the highly acclaimed television series *The Sopranos*, viewers saw a depiction of the trauma that can result from facing a parent's psychopathology. Mafia boss Tony Soprano is in psychotherapy for help with his panic attacks. In the first episode, viewers meet his mother, Livia, and it soon becomes clear that she is cold, cruel, and narcissistic—clear, that is, to the viewer but not to Tony. Despite abundant evidence of his mother's inability to love, Tony remains loyal, defending his mother to his therapist, Dr. Melfi, as just a "tough old bird." He repeatedly tries to offer comfort to his mother, who systematically rejects and demeans his efforts. As the season progresses it becomes clear that not only does Livia not love her son, but she hates him. While the immediate cause of Livia's resentment is the fact that Tony forced her to move to a retirement home, it is apparent that her mothering was always riddled with exploitation and violence.

Lurking in the background throughout the season is the possibility that Tony's uncle "Junior" will have him assassinated. It gradually becomes clear that Livia is a co-conspirator in the plot to murder her own son. After the "hit" on Tony is unsuccessful, Tony goes to see his therapist, who suggests he is warding off his unconscious awareness that Livia was behind the assassination attempt. Tony erupts in a rage, overturns the coffee table and physically threatens Dr. Melfi, saying, "Are you telling me that my own mother tried to have me whacked?" Tony then storms out of the office.

This scene beautifully illustrates how traumatic it is to face the reality of a parent's psychological pathology. The entire first season of *The Sopranos* can be seen as the story of a man coming face-to-face with reality, including the reality of having had a terrifying and destructive family. Most of us, of course, don't have mothers who want us dead, but we likely do have mothers who might have been psychologically impaired in ways that we, like Tony, refuse to face. Better to blame ourselves. Tony works hard to externalize his demons but remains tragic in the knowledge that ultimately they lie within himself.

Children are highly motivated to deny their own innocence in order to retain some semblance of parental virtue, protection, and love. Unfortunately, this denial of innocence continues into adult social life and is mirrored by a similar denial of broader truths. Most Americans internalize the belief that they live in a meritocracy—the assumption that everyone is responsible for his or her own social position and that therefore those who feel discontented, marginalized, devalued, or thwarted have only themselves to blame. Our culture promotes an ethos of personal responsibility in which upward mobility supposedly reflects intrinsic worth and virtue while social and economic hardships reflect a personal failure. Despite overwhelming evidence that economic mobility has more to do with class, race, and the gender one is born into than with personal ability, people have an overwhelming need to assume personal responsibility for their lot.

The damage done by this irrational belief in a meritocracy is immediately obvious in the depressive self-blaming that occurs among "downsized" workers after a corporation moves its operations overseas. Laid off workers frequently feel depressed and personally inadequate despite the obvious fact that they weren't responsible for their unemployment. Or consider the reaction of people who lost money in the burst of the stock market bubble in 2000. Most of my patients and friends who lost money found some way to blame themselves. One told me that she "knew" that she should get out early but got lazy. Another complained that he had told his broker to sell but hadn't followed up with him aggressively enough. And still another confessed that he was to blame because he just went along with the "herd mentality." Regardless of the details of each individual's investment decisions, the fact that each felt that his or her losses were a result of an individual failure of some kind, rather than the fact that they were part of a collective phenomenon, speaks to the fact that people simply cannot tolerate being innocent victims of forces beyond their control. Just as children can't face being helpless victims of parental pathology, so, too, adults can't face being helpless and innocent victims of social pathology. We keep trying to blame others, but in our deepest core, cannot really absolve ourselves.

The one class of people who everyone agrees is innocent, however, is children who are victims of sexual abuse. While we may not be able to view ourselves as victims deserving of protection, we have no trouble affording this status to sexually innocent children. There can be no doubt whatsoever that the sexual abuse of a child by an adult is undeserved. The child molester is doing something that is so unnatural, so forbidden, that even the most harshly zealous advocate of personal responsibility has to admit that these particular little victims didn't deserve what they got. The pedophile is crossing a universally accepted boundary, motivated entirely by his own need, and corrupting the virginal innocence of a child.

The same cannot be said for our attitudes toward the child victims of emotional deprivation and neglect. In these cases, the traumas seem more abstract and general. Most important, however, is that such treatment seems more ordinary, a childhood hardship that its victims ought to be able to rise above. We mute our awareness of and outrage over childhood neglect by thinking such things as, "Well, I had it tough, too, but I managed to survive." Moreover, some people minimize or dismiss problems of attachment, abandonment, and neglect altogether.

Not so with sexual abuse. The lines are, for once, clearly drawn. We unconsciously long for situations in which we can feel such moral clarity because when it comes to our own victimization, whether in our families or society, our consciences won't let us be clear about anything. We cannot experience ourselves as innocent, even if we were and are. Instead, we develop an enchanted view of the sexual innocence of childhood in order to locate a part of ourselves in a place that is finally above reproach.

Should Healthy Sexuality Be Controlled?

Pedophilia is only the most controversial and provocative example of how sexual behavior that looks simple on the outside is actually extremely complex on the inside, and is only the most obvious example of how much sex can be a lightning rod for a vast array of social, political, and psychological projections. When we lock up pedophiles and throw away the key, our conscious aim may simply be to make our children safer, but I see little evidence that such is the case. Children—and adults for that matter—do need protection from all sorts of dangers in our society, one of which may be child molesters, but the current penchant for punishment and incarceration does not seem to me to be making people feel any safer. Instead, the more we try to control dangerous sexual behavior, rather than attempt to understand and change its root causes, the less safe we become. The more that sexuality is suppressed, the more disturbed individuals seek out forbidden forms of it.

We need to take a collective breath and calmly look at what exactly we think we're controlling when we attempt to censor and regulate sexuality. What do we think we'll accomplish by, for example, censoring sexually oriented websites in public libraries or telling sexually active teenagers that even condoms are not a good form of birth control. Sexual desires don't disappear because we tell them to. Many teenagers will continue to have sex, although we run the risk of leaving them unprepared for the experience by refusing to discuss it meaningfully in our schools and families. Internet use is expanding at a rapid rate. Attempts to censor it by criminalizing its content or denying access to it in libraries looks more and more like closing the barn door after the horses have already run away.

We have to balance our obligation to protect children from sexual harm with our moral obligation to treat everyone, perpetrator and victim, as worthy of empathy and respect. That means we have to get pedophiles off the street and into treatment programs that are much better than those we have today. It means we have to understand better the psychological and social forces that create sex offenders and try to correct them earlier in their development. It means we have to be able to have frank discussions with our children about potential threats to their sexual well-being, teach them how to defend themselves against such threats, but not worsen their vulnerability by exaggerating the dangers of sexuality. The sense that many young people get from adults about sex is that while it feels great, it's really a radioactive device that will either ruin their lives or drive them into the fallout shelters of fear and repression.

Healthy sexuality exists. It is not intrinsically heterosexual, confined to marriage, or even inextricably tied to intimacy. It may be any or all of these things, but it may not. It is always consenting and it should always involve a basic respect for the other person in real life. It is never shameful. It is always safe, both physically and emotionally. And it should enhance its practitioners' self-esteem and never threaten it. It is incompatible with pedophilia, incest, rape, or coercion of any kind, and it is not a substitute for caretaking or love. Families need to convey this possibility to children. Other social institutions should reinforce it as well. Ignorance, repression, and shame are a sure recipe for disaster.

The Value of Difference

S EVERAL YEARS INTO OUR MARRIAGE, my wife and I were having conflicts in which each of us was feeling unappreciated and emotionally deprived in the relationship. We came to understand that each of us was showing love in the way that each of us would most appreciate receiving love. My wife felt most loved when I used language to express it, and I felt most loved when she showed it through actions. I realized that I was showing her what I felt, that she was telling me what she felt, and neither of us felt appreciated or loved in the process. In other words, we were loving each other as if we each had the same needs and vulnerabilities—a failure of empathy that led to considerable frustration. One of the most important sources of pain and suffering in relationships is the difficulty understanding a partner's difference.

The differences between men and women are often problematic, but nowhere is the problem more acute than in the bedroom. Over and over again, sexual problems in relationships turn out to stem from fundamental misunderstandings about the meanings of each other's sexual needs and worries. The women's movement of the 1960s and 1970s brought women's sexuality out of the closet where it had been relegated by a repressive patriarchal culture that was afraid of it. Unfortunately, male sexuality has always seemed transparent and, if anything, *too* obvious and thus has never been subject to the type of deep and sympathetic exploration that feminists provided for female sexuality. As a result, misunderstandings, projections, and distortions persist, bringing discord and suffering into the erotic lives of both men and women.

Male sexuality is not simple. It is not primarily driven by hormones, nor is it intrinsically stronger than that of women. At their deepest level, most men don't see women as things, conquests, or simply means to a sexual end. Most men don't hate women but worry about them; they don't feel superior but often inferior; and they aren't irresponsible but often feel too responsible. Men may actually have more power than women, but they usually feel as if they have less. They may appear not to need women, but are more likely to feel secretly as if their needs are bottomless. The real reason that men sometimes put women down is to avoid feeling put down themselves. The real reason that some men abandon women is to to avoid feeling abandoned. A central purpose of this book has been to debunk myths about the male libido, to look underneath its surface appearance to discover its roots in the special fears and longings buried in the male psyche.

Men themselves rarely understand their own sexuality, a fact that contributes to the misconceptions that women have about them. Men are not only less willing in general to be introspective than women, but are also more likely to feel shame about the ways that their sexual preferences are based on emotions deemed weak, or on feelings like guilt, worry, helplessness, and inferiority. Further, men are particularly ashamed of fantasies that appear to violate traditional masculine norms. Such embarrassment contributes to a general fear of self-disclosure in men and leads them to shut down in conversations with women about sexual matters. One of the great potential benefits of the theory of sexual arousal presented here is that not only can women come to understand their male partners better, but also men can reduce their shame about their own sexuality.

Male sexuality has to contend with special versions of two powerful emotional states: guilt and loneliness. Women share these feelings but in a different way. To the extent that masculinity has to involve a rejection of femininity, men feel both hyper-responsible for women and have difficulty connecting with them. Such painful feelings are highly personal but also profoundly social. Consider the central psychic role of guilt. Our culture contributes mightily to its intensity and repressiveness. For example, we devalue old age and celebrate youth, prejudicial attitudes that lend a certain reality to the survivor guilt that people feel about surpassing their elders, about leaving them behind. And our societal ideal of individualism further accentuates separation guilt because it contains the expectation that children will move away from home, start their own families, and "make it" in society without the help of kinship networks. In our culture, guilt is regularly evoked and exacerbated by the drumbeat about independence and the virtue of leaving one's family. The "good life" in our culture is based on separation and autonomy, not on familial or community engagement, and such an ethos makes us more vulnerable to feeling disloyal and guilty about excluding loved ones from our lives.

Consider what might happen if our society provided families with more help in raising children, more opportunities for love and attachment than one or even two caretakers can provide. What if we were able to introduce more balance and flexibility into our ideals of masculinity and femininity? Perhaps then we could create families in which boys no longer had to push away from their mothers with such rigidity and girls no longer had to feel so guilty about being strong. Men might feel less burdened with responsibility and feel less inclined to use their sexuality to avoid it. Grown women might feel less survivor guilt about having pleasure and might be able to enjoy more varied and less inhibited forms of it with greater impunity. The result might then be a more liberated and healthy type of sexual connectedness between the sexes.

As we've seen, men today are lonelier than ever, and such isolation is fertile ground for a growing interest in pornography and Internet sex. Men today are not only isolated by the type of masculinity that they developed growing up, a masculinity that seemed to require an especially forceful push way from their mothers, but they are isolated merely by adapting to their normal social role. My patient Joe, who seemed to be addicted to pornography and prostitutes, grew up feeling quite alone in his family. And yet there are millions of Joes who work every day at jobs in which they are cut off from peers, who go home to families who don't know their neighbors, and raise children without the benefit of the extended families and support of past generations. These men are subject to a type of everyday loneliness and isolation that is so normal few would complain about it. These same men, if they don't turn to drugs or alcohol for relief, seek out a male culture of camaraderie based on objectifying women, or have affairs with women for whom they feel no responsibility, or spend hours with their porn collections and computer monitors fantasizing about being connected to women who want nothing more than to make them happy. Their wives suffer the same types of isolation, of course, although women tend to be more embedded in supportive relationships than men. But the forces that drive men apart do the same to women.

The solution to the problem of alienation in our society is to recognize that both men and women need to feel connected, need communities in which they feel recognized and safe, and need to have work in which they feel they're making a contribution to something bigger than themselves. Both sexes need lives that are more engaged with other people while at the same time embracing the freedom to be selfishly pleasure seeking. Sex, after all, is about being separate and joined at the same time. The fact that men tend to emphasize the former and women the latter is not an irreducible fact of gender, but the result of asymmetries in childrearing and socialization. But more than that, such tensions reflect the fact that in our society as a whole we don't know how to be involved with one another without feeling burdened or selfishly indulgent without feeling guilty. If we can solve this problem on a societal level, it will go a long way to solving it in the bedroom.

However, it won't go all the way. Sex will always be complicated. Sexual fantasies are universal, arising as they do from the need to transcend feelings of guilt, worry, rejection, and helplessness. Such feelings, while taking destructive forms in many of our lives because of the pathologies in our families of origin and in our culture, are a part of the human condition. We grow up especially attuned to the feelings of our caretakers, necessarily sensitive to signs of their unhappiness and to the potential for the loss of their love. Therefore, who could imagine a childhood absent *any* feelings of guilt or rejection? Sexual desire will, then, always have to navigate a path through the chilling effects of these feelings and will always use sexual fantasy to do so. And to the extent that gender differences, however mitigated, will always exist, there will most likely always be differences in how these fantasies play out.

We should be grateful for and appreciate these differences as well. Difference creates the essential mystery and dynamic tension inherent in healthy love and passion. But we need to strip sexuality of the shame that so often clings to it and seek to communicate to one another more clearly what we want and why.

Whether or not we're able to effect the broad social changes necessary to create a world that doesn't regularly produce distortions in masculinity and femininity, then, there is an urgent need for greater understanding between the sexes.

Sex will always be complicated for both men and women. Thankfully, it is simple to enjoy. Understanding its dynamics will never put a damper on sexual pleasure, but failing to do so can make such pleasure more difficult and painful to share.

The benefits of understanding are incalculable. We can analyze the meaning of our sexual desire while still surrendering to its passion. We can appreciate the centrality of safety in sexual arousal and still feel the thrill of the unexpected in the bedroom. Leonardo da Vinci once said, "The noblest pleasure is the joy of understanding." The power of the human imagination to rescue us from our limitations can be appreciated, analyzed, and embraced without reducing it to theorems. In so doing, we not only become wiser but also more human.

Index

abortion, 134
American Psychological Association
   (APA), 134, 135
audio and video streaming, 45–46

Blink (Gladwell), 15
breasts: Internet sexual
   experimentation, 54; sexual
   markers, 41
bulletin boards, 46, 51
Bumstead, Dagwood, 42, 125

cases/clinical examples: addiction to
   pornography and prostitutes, 8–11,
   42–43, 44, 45, 46–47, 48; being held
   down by partner, 114; bondage and
   safe arousal, 16, 18; breast fixation
   and sexual mutuality, 35–37, 40;
   breasts and pleasure, 16; cybersex
   fantasy life, 50; cybersex infidelity,
   57–59; cybersex sexual addiction,
   51–53, 56; fantasy nymphet and
   aging wife, 83–88; girl-on-girl sex,
   17; helpless/passive partner, 27–29;
   husband's hostility and
   pornography, 104–5; inability to
   tolerate Internet transitional space,
   49; in-charge/"top" sexual partner,
   18; Internet and escalation of sexual

experimentation, 54; Lolita figures,
   16–17; loss of control and arousal,
   37–40; mutual lack of desire, 67–68;
   overly sensitive couple, 67; parental
   abandonment and pathogenic
   beliefs, 13; perceived emotional
   detachment during sex, 34;
   pornographic "facials," 17;
   receptive/"bottom" partner, 18; sex
   talk and arousal, 114; sexual activity
   as barometer, 43; sexual
   chemistry/sexual attraction, 78–79;
   sexually "uptight" wife, 56–57; sex
   with two women, 17–18; triangle of
   infidelity, 71–77; understanding
   pornography use, 114–15;
   undressing/stripping women, 17;
   vaginal lubrication and sexual
   desire, 68–71; women in high heels,
   18
Catholic Church, 88, 90, 91, 137
chat rooms, 47, 51
child pornography, 130
children/childhood: abuse and neglect,
   61, 132–33, 138–41; attuned to
   caretakers' moods, 13–14, 24,
   139–40; dealing with isolation and
   loneliness, 34; femininity task for
   girls, 21, 25–29; forming pathogenic

151

CPSIA information can be obtained at www.ICGtesting.com
Printed in the USA
BVOW021232200612

293122BV00005B/1/P